T0281801

EDUCARING FROM THE HEART

Inviting readers on a journey of self-reflection, *Educaring from the Heart* offers an approach to education that places care, empathy, and compassion at the core of the educator's role.

Within the book, readers are introduced to the principles underpinning educaring from the heart and encouraged to consider their own positionality when reflecting on the role they play in supporting both the learning and wellbeing of their students. Practical exercises are woven throughout to allow the reader to critically engage with how they understand themselves and their values as educators, and how this then shapes their wellbeing and practices in the classroom.

The book is divided into three distinct sections:

- The "I" as Educator
- The "Us" as Educator and Student
- The "We" as Cocreators for Wellbeing

With a focus on nurturing wellbeing and learning within the classroom, as well as the power of co-creativity, this book is an essential read for educators seeking to re/discover their purpose within education and to foster positive outcomes for their students.

Deirdre McGillicuddy is an Assistant Professor in Education at UCD School of Education, University College Dublin, Ireland. She is a Froebel-trained primary school teacher and has 25 years' experience working in education and contributing to programmes preparing educators to work in early years settings, primary and secondary schools. Deirdre employs wellbeing practices at the heart of her own teaching/pedagogy for which she was awarded a UCD Teaching and Learning award (2020) and was a finalist in the ACEEU Triple E European Awards as Fast Forward Entrepreneurship Educator of the Year (2022).

EDUCARING FROM THE HEART

How to Nurture Your Wellbeing and Rediscover Your Purpose in Education

Deirdre McGillicuddy

Routledge
Taylor & Francis Group

LONDON AND NEW YORK

Cover design image: Illustration by Mick Wallace.

First published 2024
by Routledge
4 Park Square, Milton Park, Abingdon, Oxon OX14 4RN

and by Routledge
605 Third Avenue, New York, NY 10158

Routledge is an imprint of the Taylor & Francis Group, an informa business

© 2024 Deirdre McGillicuddy

British Library Cataloguing-in-Publication Data
A catalogue record for this book is available from the British Library

ISBN: 978-1-032-71818-7 (hbk)
ISBN: 978-1-032-71787-6 (pbk)
ISBN: 978-1-032-71819-4 (ebk)

DOI: 10.4324/9781032718194

Typeset in Interstate
by SPi Technologies India Pvt Ltd (Straive)

I dedicate this book to my Mam, Monica McGillicuddy, who always encouraged me to reach for the stars and who showed me the true meaning and power of love, care, empathy, and compassion. This book is also dedicated to all the educators, pupils, and students I have had the privilege to meet on my own journey through education. They inspire me to do better and continuously teach me about the importance and value of putting care at the heart of my own work as an educator.

CONTENTS

Preface   ix
Acknowledgements   x

1 **Educaring: To the Heart of the Matter**   1

PART 1: THE "I" AS EDUCATOR   7

2 **The Educator Backpack**   9

3 **Our Values**   24

4 **Our *Why***   32

5 **Our Wellbeing**   45

PART 2: THE "US" AS EDUCATOR AND STUDENT   63

6 **Nurturing the Individual**   65

7 **Compassionate Education**   76

8 **The Power of Relational Pedagogy**   86

9 **Empowering Voices**   92

PART 3: THE "WE" AS COCREATORS FOR WELLBEING   103

10 Cocreating Heart-Full Education   105

11 Creativity for Wellbeing   115

**PART 4: UNITING "I", "WE", AND "US" - A FRAMEWORK
FOR EDUCARING FROM THE HEART**   123

12 A Framework for Educaring from the Heart   125

Index   *134*

PREFACE

Education is one of the most fulfilling and rewarding professions in our societies. It is the foundation stone upon which we build our communities, playing a critical role in shaping who we are as citizens and how we interact with the world around us. As educators we continuously give of ourselves as we navigate the complexity of the learning environment. The global intensification of time and workload demands across education systems has impacted educators' sense of wellbeing and purpose as they grapple with the chronic pressures of their work. This book shines a light into the deep crevices of education to explore the impact chronic overwork is having on the wellbeing of educators and learners across our education systems. It proposes a countercultural approach to education, calling for an urgent slowing down in order to place greater emphasis on care, empathy and compassion as core values to educaring from the heart. This approach takes the reader on a journey from understanding the educator as an individual (the "I"), to the crucial partnership between educator and learner (the "We"), finishing with the ultimate coming together in community to co-create learning (the "Us"). Each stage of the educaring from the heart journey interrogates and problematises the complexities of working in our contemporary education systems in order to make sense of why educators feel the way they do. While this book cannot directly solve the challenges facing educators across the continuum of education – from early childhood settings, schooling environments, and in higher and further educational contexts – it seeks to provide a framework to re/focus our attention on the importance of care, empathy, and compassion within and through our education systems. This starts with caring for and about educators. Educaring from the heart is an invitation to nurture your wellbeing and rediscover your purpose in education.

ACKNOWLEDGEMENTS

To my amazingly talented, creative, and wonderful children Oisín, Fionn and Róise - you are the moonlight to lift me, the starlight to guide me, and the sunlight to warm my soul. I am so blessed to have you all walk beside me on our journey through life together.

To my best friend and life partner, Mick - you are always unwavering and solid in your love and support, especially in times when I doubt or question myself. You are my rock and I am so grateful for all you do for me and for our family.

To my family - you are always there supporting and encouraging me as I navigate my journey to the stars. Ava and Aaron - you inspire me with your joy, fun, and creativity.

To my friends, old and new - you catch me when I fall, encourage and inspire me, and show me the healing power of deeply connected relationships and coming together in community.

To my mentor who helped me see the light, break the shackles, find my voice, and guided me down the road less travelled. For this, I am forever grateful.

This book is from my heart to yours.
Grá mo chroí sibh go léir

1 Educaring

To the Heart of the Matter

Educaring from the heart proposes a pedagogic approach that places care, empathy, and compassion at the heart of the education system to nurture wellbeing and contribute to the flourishing and thriving of our wider societies. Educaring from the heart is, at times, countercultural in its principles, requiring a slowing down to nurture wellbeing and creativity in education. It has become increasingly evident as I progress through my own journey in education that educaring from the heart matters. It is the fulcrum around which our education systems, our schools and educational institutions, our classrooms/learning environments, and our relationships should be built. It provides the critical scaffolding required to nurture the humanity at the heart of education, the arterial connection between individuals who cocreate spaces for teaching, learning, and thriving within our education systems. Healthy, nurturing and heart-full education systems are the cornerstone of ensuring we have thriving societies where care, empathy, and compassion are at the core of how we interact with our fellow citizens and the wider world around us.

Educaring from the heart begins with intentionality. It is a conscious decision to place care, empathy, and compassion at the core of your work as an educator. It takes courage and vulnerability to create safe spaces within which both educator and learner can come together, take risks, and engage in an authentic and genuine way. It requires openness and trust where failure and mistakes are acknowledged as key milestones in the educational journey. It challenges the hegemonic distribution of power typically experienced in and across our education systems, and positions educators and learners as partners in a journey of cocreating the teaching and learning experience.

Educaring from the heart empowers learners and educators to engage more meaningfully in/through/with pedagogy. It is through this process of cocreation that the barriers that often exist between educator and learner are challenged, eroded, and transformed to allow a more open and meaningful engagement through the pedagogic encounter. Mutual understanding, respect, and acknowledgement is key,

DOI: 10.4324/9781032718194-1

allowing both learner and educator to express their authentic selves while engaging in the learning process. When we express our authentic self in education, we can take risks and learn about the world and the ways in which it shapes and molds us. To be seen and accepted as our authentic self is the most powerful and transformative potential of education. Valuing each learner for who they are opens limitless transformative possibilities, not only for the individual, but also for our wider societies. It empowers a sense of authentic action whereby individuals themselves build a sense of confidence and agency around who they are as key contributors both within the learning environment and beyond. To empower the learner is to empower citizenship within our increasingly complex globalized world.

Educaring from the heart is not just an aspirational musing on how we can progress our educational interactions and enhance pedagogy for the future – it is a call to action. We live in an increasingly neoliberal world, where our focus in education can often be distracted by delivering outputs (such as exam results, numeracy and literacy attainment levels, and degree or further education programmes) at the cost to the holistic development of the individual. Such holistic development occurs predominantly through the symbiotic relationship between educator and learner, with both individuals changed through the educational and pedagogic encounter. The intensity of change occurring within our world, experienced both in person (in interaction with others) and virtually (through digital devices), places pressure on our education systems to be immediately responsive and dynamic in addressing the complex challenges that arise within our societies. Such challenges will continue to be omnipresent within our world – and as such, reflected within our education systems – as we seek to support our fellow humans who are impacted by climate change, war, migration, food and energy crises, and political and economic turmoil. Educaring from the heart imbues education with values of care, empathy, and compassion, and is fundamental to contributing to the re/formation of citizens who can respond to humanitarian challenges in compassionate and empathic ways.

Care, empathy, and compassion are the foundational principles upon which educaring from the heart is conceptualized and understood. To be cared for, and to care about and for other individuals is at the core of what it means to be human. Without experiencing and expressing care we cannot have a sense of who we are. It is fundamental to our psychological development, our positive sense of wellbeing and our overall health outcomes. Empathy is to understand and share in the feelings of another and cannot be done in the absence of being able to care. Feelings play an important role in the expression of self, our values, and how we see the world around us. Experiencing empathy in education teaches pupils/students how to be empathetic to individuals as they express their authentic selves in the learning environment. By experiencing empathy children and young people learn how to be empathic. Such empathetic engagement in/through/with

Figure 1.1 Educaring from the heart - care, empathy, and compassion

pedagogy is symbiotically beneficial for both learner and educator, etching the practice of empathy into everyday practices and engagements in their lives. The nurturing of compassion arises through our response to empathy - how we react and respond to an individual to help or support them. This interaction between care, empathy, and compassion is fundamental to educaring from the heart (Figure 1.1).

Educaring from the heart is realized through the the relational power between the educator and learner as they experience care, empathy, and compassion in the educational setting. It is vital that educators are equipped with the knowledge, language, and awareness that will enable them to educate from the heart, passing the core principles and actions of care, empathy, and compassion on to learners and contributing to a ripple impact on our wider societies. It is only when students experience care, empathy, and compassion in their own educational experiences that deep and meaningful learning can truly begin. Indeed, it is only when our education systems care for the souls of their students that those students can then go on and care for the souls of their fellow citizens in and across our societies.

This book explores the art of educaring from the heart, which starts with you, the "I" as educator, teacher, mentor, role model, and imperfect human. Education is one of the most challenging professions because there is nowhere to hide. You stand, vulnerable and courageous, in front of other humans, giving all of yourself to the educational encounter as mediated by pedagogy. This encounter demands mental, physical, relational, and emotional energy in order to ensure it is successful in content and delivery. Indeed, it could be argued that educating, by its very nature, is a sharing and giving of your heart, whether consciously or subconsciously. Awakening consciousness around this heart-filled encounter is especially important to contributing to a more empathetic and compassionate education system, one that is flexible and responsive to wider societal challenges and issues.

Given the complexity of the educational encounter and the demands on educators to ensure efficacy in learner engagement, the decision to enter the profession is often underpinned by ideals and principles of helping people (especially children and young people) to grow, learn, and thrive in their lives. While the common argument is that educating is a vocation, the skills required to teach effectively are complex and play a critical role in ensuring that our education systems flourish and thrive at an effective level. Indeed, educators are the most important factor for ensuring highly effective education systems. Hence, investing in their education and continuous professional development is vital. The curriculum for professional educators (such as Initial Teacher Education) is foundational to the re/formation of their professional identities, as well as the skills, competencies, and knowledge they will bring to their respective educational roles (from early childhood to higher education) and learning environments (early childhood settings, classrooms, lecture theatres, and so on). As such, education programmes for professional educators are critical strategic partners for creating an education system committed to educaring from the heart. Indeed, educaring from the heart should guide our formal and informal education systems, from early years to lifelong learning, and including informal educational contexts.

As the first step on this journey through educaring from the heart, I invite you to re/consider your purpose in education. The first, and perhaps the most critical question to reflect upon is *what has put education into your own heart?* We rarely take the time in the busyness of our professional lives to stop and consider how we came to a vocation that plays such a vital role in our societies. Perhaps you are considering becoming an educator and are not sure yet whether it is a path you wish to take. Maybe you are in a transitional phase in your professional life and considering whether you want to continue as educator. Perhaps you are engaged now in learning to become a professional educator and are not sure it is for you. Use the following exercise to help you to consider what has put education into your heart, why it is that you are an educator. What has called you to this role? The following exercise in Figure 1.2 is an invitation to reflect on and consider your motivation to be an educator.

What has put education into
your heart?

Figure 1.2 Exercise: What has put education into your heart?

Educaring from the Heart

Capture your thoughts & feelings here

Part 1: The "I" as Educator

2 The Educator Backpack

We come to the educational encounter with our educator backpacks, informed and shaped by how we understand who we are in the world around us. Our educator identities have been re/formed and shaped by our families of origin, our childhood experiences, and our own experiences in school. As we progress through the education system, our experiences of success and failure, our social worlds, and the people with whom we interact, all shape our identities as educators. Also important is our belief systems, our educational philosophies, which have been shaped and re/formed in initial educator education, our experiences with children and young people in education systems, and the school/institutional culture within which we work. Essentially, our educator identities are shaped by our humanity - our strengths, limitations, successes, failures, relationships, and sense of who we are in the wider world and the classroom.

A backpack helps us carry objects. It has a physical presence on our back. We carry the weight of the backpack. Externally, it has a shape and a design we have chosen when we purchase it. However, we may not be aware of what is actually in the backpack until we open it, rummage through it, and find all its contents, even those hidden in the dark crevices of the stitching. Consider a child's school bag when they return home, just before a holiday break - jammed to the brim with their work sent home by their teacher, remnants from lunch boxes or treats tucked away out of sight, little toys secretly hidden to comfort them throughout the school day, and message cards or paper notes placed into a small pocket to share and exchange with their friends. It is not until you open the school bag and empty the contents that you see and witness the volume and variety that is held within. The greatest fear in that moment of emptying the backpack is finding something you didn't expect or even know was there, such as a squashed banana in the depths of the bag.

Building on the concept of the invisible knapsack developed by Peggy McIntosh (1998), educaring from the heart invites educators to unpack the educator backpack they bring to the educational encounter. This backpack is laden with all the

DOI: 10.4324/9781032718194-3

parts of who we are as imperfect human beings. The contents held within our educator backpacks are shaped by the intersection and interaction of the spheres that are re/forming our understandings of who we are in the world. These spheres include our family of origin, cultural worlds, childhoods, professional and personal relationships, social worlds, health and wellbeing, family circumstances, educational opportunities and experiences, socioeconomic influences, professional experiences, and working culture. While these spheres intersect and interact within and across each other, they are dynamic and ever changing in response to the unfolding of our own life journeys. No two life journeys are ever the same. They are unique to each individual. As such, our education systems are constantly re/formed by and through the complex negotiation between the re/formational spheres of both educator and learner as they navigate their life journeys (Figure 2.1).

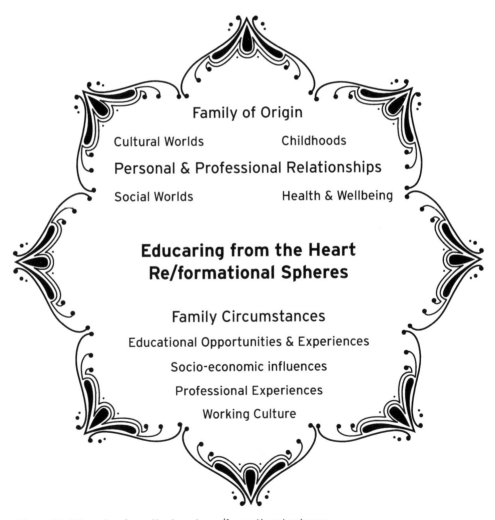

Figure 2.1 Educaring from the heart - re/formational spheres

RRD

(POD)

Do Not Dot
See Lead

While each of these spheres are distinctive, having their own specific and unique characteristics, they interact to shape and re/form how we understand our identities as educators. They have a profound impact on our capacity to educare from the heart when engaging with our pupils and students.

Family of Origin It goes without saying that the family into which we were born has a profound impact on how we see and understand ourselves in the world. Our early childhood experiences are foundational for our social, emotional, and psychological development. Our family of origin shapes our early childhood experiences, contributing to our socioemotional and psychological development. Much of the scientific evidence within the field of childhood development identifies the importance of positive childhood experiences in shaping neural pathways in the brain that contribute to positive socioemotional and psychological development. As an educator perhaps you had little opportunity to consider the role of your family of origin, not only in terms of your own personal development and growth, but also in terms of how you understand yourself and interact with the world around you. Specifically, it is important to consider how your own experiences within your family of origin shape your interactions with children and young people in the learning environment. How has your experience in your family of origin informed your practice as an educator? How has it shaped your approach the relational aspects of teaching? How has it shaped your understanding of how family is defined and expressed? How has it shaped your interpretation of learner responses in the classroom, as they navigate their learning experiences? To educare from the heart, we must be aware of what we experienced within our families of origin and how that shapes our own approach to care, empathy, and compassion in the classroom. It begins with awareness. It begins with our own personal family experiences.

Cultural Worlds Our family experiences are shaped by the culture influencing the nature of their practices, lifeworld perspectives, and understandings of interactions and relationships. We occupy spaces defined by culture(s) that are increasingly diverse and multifaceted in characteristics and expectations. The cultural understandings we accrue as we navigate our lives inform and shape how we interact with learners in our classroom. Our cultural worldview shapes our own expectations for our students and is based on our own cultural understanding of what it means to be a learner in the classroom. At times, this can result in misrecognition or misunderstanding between cultures, which can manifest as unconscious bias, whereby educators subconsciously and unintentionally hold different expectations for learners from different cultural backgrounds. Such misrecognition can have profound impact on children and young people, shaping their educational trajectories and their experience within the learning environment. As educators, it is vital that we identify and acknowledge our own cultural worldview as it shapes our practices and expectations in the classroom. Furthermore, it is imperative to reflect upon any unconscious bias we may hold, which shapes how we engage with our pupils and students. Such reflection is especially important as our globalised societies become more culturally and socially diverse. To educare from the heart is to recognise our own cultural biases and to embrace cultural diversity in and across our education systems.

Childhoods Our experience of childhood is foundational for shaping who we are in adulthood. Childhood marks the most critical stage in our brain development and growth. It is the time when we form ideas of who we are, based on the experiences we have in our life worlds. Our neural pathways and brain development are shaped and defined by these experiences, which lay the foundation blocks of our characteristics, expectations, and relationships as we develop into adulthood. Childhood shapes adulthood, both in positive and negative ways. We learn how to be in the world during our childhoods, distilled in the contexts within which we live and interact. Although our childhoods do not define who we are as adults, it is fundamental to who we are as humans. Our childhoods are embodied within us as we journey through our lives. Our identity is constantly in flux, moving and responding to the experiences we have as we navigate our lifeworld. Identity is not fixed, rather it constantly re/shaped and re/formed through our relationships with others and the world around us. Childhood provides the conditions to explore, take risks, fail successfully, and re/form or identities as we grow and develop. Developmental psychologist Abraham Maslow (1943) situates the stages of growth in humans within a hierarchy of needs. The five stages of this hierarchy are physiological, safety, belonging and love, esteem and self-actualisation. Importantly, each stage on this hierarchy must be realised by the individual before they can progress to the next one. Childhood ideally provides the conditions required to allow children to grow through these different stages of development and attain the level of self-actualisation, which is also known as the realisation of the individual's full potential. Although we may be familiar with Maslow's hierarchy of needs in education, have you ever considered where you are in terms of your own psychological development as measured against Maslow's hierarchy of needs? Perhaps engaging in such an exercise will provide a deeper understanding of who you are, and how your own childhood development has re/formed who you are as an educator in the classroom today. Most importantly, growth is a part of the human condition, so we can continue to nurture our roots as humans, grow, and develop as we challenge ourselves and our understanding of and response to the world around us.

Personal and Professional Relationships Education is deeply embedded within a complex network of relationships. In fact, education cannot exist in a relational vacuum. Positive relationships are absolutely essential to ensuring education is effective. Our personal and professional relationships inform our relational approaches and practices as educators with our pupils and students. Our repertoire of relational approaches is informed in and through the relationships we have experienced both successfully and unsuccessfully in our personal and professional lives. As educators, we are constantly learning how best to approach the relational dimensions in our classrooms as informed by the diverse and unique individuals and pupils/students we have the privilege to encounter along our own professional and personal journeys. We carry these relational skills in our educator backpack, drawing upon them on a daily basis, particularly in situations where relational crises can arise, needing to be addressed in those in-the-moment situations. Educaring from the heart invites the educator to deeply integrate care, empathy, and compassion into the relational approaches they nurture within the learning environment.

Social Worlds The social world we occupy shapes our perspective of the world around us, hence shaping who we are as educators. It is within these social worlds that our perspectives and understandings of what it means to be human are defined. That is to say, we are shaped and re/formed in and through our interactions with those around us. Our social worlds are contextualised and defined through our relationships with the people who occupy them. Shared values and perspectives contribute to defining social worlds, where individuals can be included/excluded based on their alignment with the dominant views within a group. As humans, we consciously and subconsciously carry these views and perspectives into our work in education. They shape our work as educators both in terms of how we understand and interact at systemic (in schools/education settings) and individual levels (with children/young people and the wider educational community). It is important to reflect on the role of our own social worlds in shaping who we are as educators in the classroom and beyond.

Health and Wellbeing Much research has highlighted the profound impact teacher/educator wellbeing has on the effectiveness of their teaching in the classroom. The teacher is the most influential factor for school effectiveness and improvement. As such, teachers/educators hold limitless possibilities for positive transformation across our education system, yet such potential is often limited by a multitude of complex factors that negatively impact their wellbeing. We often hear the maternalistic phrase, "happy mother, happy child". The same can be said of educators. Being content in our roles, with a clear vision of our purpose, is critical to nurturing our wellbeing as teachers and educators. Yet curriculum overload, the devaluing of the role of educator in society, initiative burnout, intensification of socioemotional challenges evident in classrooms, complexities of needs among students, and increased monitoring and surveillance has directly impacted educators' health and wellbeing. Educators' health and wellbeing affects the nature of interactions with learners. Our mental, physical, and social health play an important role in our expression as educators. It is vital that we pay attention to these three aspects of health in order to effectively engage as educators in our classrooms. Educaring from the heart starts with caring for our own hearts and health.

Family Circumstances Our economic and family circumstances shape our identities as educators. How we understand the children and young people in our classrooms is strongly influenced by how we experience and interact with children and young people in our wider families. Our position in our life journey shapes and informs who we are as educators. The familial circumstances within which we find ourselves can determine how we interact in the classroom. For example, our experiences with our own families related to childcare responsibilities can influence our assumptions, expectations, and understandings of the complexity of childhood, which young people must negotiate. Our family circumstances are made up of our family of origin, wider familial networks, and care responsibilities, which may include dependents or family members who require care support. The recognition of diversity in contemporary definitions of family challenge many of the sociohistorically normative assumptions of how families are comprised, and this is reflected in our learning environments. Educaring from the heart requires us to take an empathic and compassionate approach in recognising and embracing the diversities and complexities of family composition when working with children and young people.

Educational Opportunities and Experiences There is a reason you have been drawn to work as an educator. More often than not, the decision we make to work as educators is informed by our own educational opportunities and experiences, whether positive or negative. It may be that you had one teacher who was so inspiring and motivational, had such a positive impact on your life, that you would like to do that for children and young people. It may be that you have had an opportunity to engage in education in more informal ways (such as coaching or mentoring), which have led to your decision to become an educator. Perhaps you had a negative experience in your journey in education and are passionate about making a change so no other child or young person has a similar experience. For some it has been a direct path into education, while for others it can take much longer, with challenges and barriers along the way. There is no doubt that our own personal opportunities and experiences in education, which are varied and diverse, shape us as educators in the classroom.

Socioeconomic Influences The impact of socioeconomic influences can be seen across our societies, influencing the extent to which people can live their lives to the fullest. Socioeconomic disadvantage has been directly linked to poorer health, education, and social outcomes. Communities located in areas of socioeconomic disadvantage are more likely to experience greater social and economic unrest, which negatively impacts wellbeing and shortens life expectancy. Our socioeconomic circumstances facilitate or restrict our life opportunities, expectations, and understanding of the world around us - whether in the absence or abundance of financial capital. Socioeconomic status is also powerfully at work within our psyche, affecting our understanding of how it feels within the world around us. This can manifest as a sense of belonging within the world or as exclusion and a sense of being 'othered' and not valued within our societies. We can be blind to our privilege in the same way we can be blind to the barriers associated with socioeconomic status. Indeed, we carry our own socioeconomic perspectives and understandings with us into our role as educators working within the most intensive microcosm of life - the learning environment. We must challenge worldviews or misconceptions about socioeconomic status that we may hold as educators. Doing so is critical to developing a more empathetic and compassionate approach to education because it allows us to recognise and understand the deeply complex implications of socioeconomic circumstances for pupils/students within the learning environment, and particularly for those living in challenging circumstances.

Professional Experiences The professional experiences we accrue along our life journeys directly inform and shape our identities as educators. These can include professional experiences within and outside of education. Indeed, diversifying the population of educators across the continuum of education is critical to providing a broader spectrum of perspectives, which creates a more diverse and inclusive education system overall. The deeper and wider the spectrum and diversity of experiences across the education system, the more empathic and diverse the teaching and learning opportunities in the learning environment. Engaging with children and young people from diverse backgrounds, cultures, and socioeconomic circumstances builds our empathy and compassion as educators as we gain greater insight and perspectives into the challenges and opportunities for effective engagement within education. Diversity of experience brings with it diversity of understanding, cultivating and nurturing a more empathetic and compassionate approach to education, imbued within educaring from the heart.

Working Culture The culture within which we work shapes the nature of our interactions with our students. School and institutional culture is critical to influencing how teachers and educators engage with students. The culture nurtured and grown within an educational organisation is a fragile ecosystem within which the interactions between educators, students, and the wider school community can either thrive or deteriorate. While the educator plays the most critical role in determining educational effectiveness, it is institutional culture that determines the nature of interaction and engagement within this fragile ecosystem. The more controlling the school culture, the less space there is for educator creativity, engagement, and thriving. In contrast, the more flexible and open the school culture, the greater the opportunity for creativity and self-expression for the educator in their work with pupils/students. A critical component for promoting positive education settings is the creation of safe spaces where educators are afforded the professional trust to take risks with their students in their teaching and learning in a responsive and dynamic way. Nurturing caring, empathetic and compassionate school culture is at the very core of educaring from the heart. Empathetic and compassionate leadership is absolutely critical in this heart-full endeavour.

We carry the weight of our metaphorical educator backpacks as we engage with children, young people and adults across the continuum of education. These backpacks are comprised of those aspects of ourselves that we bring consciously and subconsciously into the classroom. We are aware of their weight, which at times can be heavier or lighter depending on the emotional load we are carrying on any given day. They shape how we view the classroom and interact with our students. Their contents include our emotional, physical, skilful, philosophical, relational, and spiritual understandings of ourselves as educators in the classroom. I refer to these as the **domains of the holistic educator**. Being aware of your own definition of each domain is especially important when educaring from the heart (Figure 2.2).

Emotional Domain The first domain in our educator backpack is the emotional. A key part of this domain is our emotional wellbeing. This domain is informed by our prior and current experiences which shape how we interact and engage within the world around us. It is important that we are aware of our emotional wellbeing, particularly when making sense of our emotional response to situations or circumstances in our professional lives. Educaring from the heart calls for us to be aware of our emotional responses and their impact on the learning environment. Awareness requires an understanding of emotional literacy to identify our own emotional responses. Indeed, emotional literacy is a critical competency to teach our pupils and students across the continuum of our education system. As educators it is critical to challenge our emotional responses and grow in emotional maturity. Equally, it is important that we establish and nurture safe spaces where our students too can reflect on their emotional responses and grow in their own emotional maturity. Educaring from the heart is educating with heart.

Physical Domain The second holistic educator domain relates to our physical wellbeing. Educating, teaching, and learning is as much a physical undertaking as it is intellectual and emotional. As such, it demands of educators to care for their physical wellbeing. Our physical bodies embody who we are as individuals. It is through our physical bodies we express our authentic selves, using voice, movement, body language, and embodied expression. As such, our physical bodies express our values, our creativity, and our understanding of who we are in the world around us. Looking after our physical self is key to nurturing our overall wellbeing, an aspect of our health that can sometimes be overlooked in the hurry and haste of

The holistic educator domains

Emotional
Emotional wellbeing
Experiences
Awareness
Literacy
Maturity
Safe spaces

Physical
Physical wellbeing
Embodied sense of self
Expression of self
Movement and self-care
Grounded presence
Body language

Skilful
Educator toolkit
Reflective practice
Professional identity
Continuous professional
development
Creativity
Student centred

Philosophical
Defining approach
Educator identity
Making sense
Signposting practices
Ethical framework
Curiosity & introspection

Relational
Authentic self
Professional self
Meaningful connection
Care and compassion
Flourishing & thriving
Positive relationships &
interactions

Spiritual
Compass
Foundation stone
Purpose & vision
Contribution to the world
Values-based approach
Sense of self

Figure 2.2 The domains of the holistic educator

our busy lives. Educating is intellectually demanding, which can sometimes result in educators living much of their time in their heads. Bringing an awareness to our physical selves is important for grounding us and bringing us into the present moment when working with children and young people in the learning environment. It also demands that we draw awareness to our body language, the medium through which we subconsciously communicate to those around us.

Skilful Domain The skills we learn, develop, and refine as we progress through our career informs our practices as educators. These skills provide us with an educator toolkit from which we draw in our daily engagement with pupils and students. A key aspect to this skilful domain is reflective practice. Effective educators continuously reflect on their practices as they interact with students, identifying gaps in knowledge and seeking out opportunities to further develop skills that enhance teaching and learning in the classroom. Our skills also inform how we re/define and re/form our professional identity as educators. Engaging in opportunities to extend our skills and improve our practices through continuous professional development requires us to engage in a process of re/forming our professional identities as educators. Nurturing and expressing your creative professional identity is also a core aspect of developing your skills as an educator shaping the learning experiences in the classroom. Educaring from the heart demands that we place students at the centre of all we do in education. Taking a student centred approach is a critical skill to ensuring more democratic and dynamic engagement with our pupils and students across the educational continuum.

Philosophical Domain The philosophical underpinning of our practice as educators informs how we teach and engage with our pupils and students. The way we approach our teaching as educators is informed by our philosophical stance. The professional development of educators has a profound impact on our educational philosophy, particularly if we were trained in a specific approach, such as Montessori or Froebel. It may be that you have and continue to shape your own philosophical perspectives based on your experiences as an educator. That perspective could include values like inclusion, equity, voice, and democracy. Embedding your own practice as an educator within a philosophical perspective shapes your identity, defining how you approach teaching and learning in your classroom. Philosophical perspectives can contribute to making sense of the complexities of the learning environment, proffering a lens through which we can understand and address issues as they arise within our practices. Our philosophical foundation provides us with clear signposts for our pedagogical approach, guiding us in the practices we employ with our pupils and students. This domain also invites us to draw on philosophical frameworks to guide us in ensuring an ethical approach as educators. Educaring from the heart calls us to begin by looking inwards with curiosity through introspection to understand who we are and how we are shaped by our philosophical stance as educators.

Relational Domain Perhaps the most powerful domain we occupy and employ as educators is the relational one. Education cannot exist in the absence of relationships. Indeed, the relational aspect of education is foundational to informing and making sense of our identities as humans as we navigate and negotiate the world around us. Education is only realised effectively through the relationships. As educators, our responsibility lies with ensuring that we can cultivate and nurture positive relationships with our pupils and students to ensure they engage in a meaningful way and achieve their fullest potential. The starting point for the relational domain is entering into relationships as your authentic self. Having the freedom to be yourself means that those around you can also have the freedom to engage in an authentic way. Of course, as an educator there is a fine balance between expressing you authentic self and presenting your professional self in front of your class. It is ethically and morally correct to bring our professional selves into the classroom. However, it is important that our professional self is presented from an authentic self. This professional self has an awareness of who they are as humans, what their needs and dreams are, what they value and treasure in their personal and professional lives, and how they wish to interact with the world around them through their relationships. It is through the intersection between the authentic and the professional self that meaningful connections can be made and grown. Such awareness enriches us as educators, benefitting our pupils and students, our wider educational communities, and the broader societies within which we build our lives. Placing care, empathy, and compassion at the heart of our authentic and professional selves is fundamental to educaring from the heart. It creates a safe space where both educators and learners can flourish and thrive. A key component of the relational domain is the nurturing of positive relationships and interactions to create the optimal conditions for effective teaching and learning, as well as for flourishing and thriving in educational settings.

Spiritual Domain The spiritual domain is perhaps one of the most overlooked aspects of our educator backpacks. Spirituality, in this context, is the way in which we understand ourselves at a deeper, more soulful level. Within this domain our spiritual selves provide us with a compass to guide our approach to living our lives. It provides a foundation stone for understanding who we are as humans. It is within the spiritual domain we derive our purpose and vision as it is situated within the greater good for society and for our world. This domain guides us in identifying and setting goals related to our intentional contribution to the world. The spiritual domain contributes to our sense of self and the world around us and affords us with an opportunity to identify and shape the values that inform our approach to working with children and young people, as well as our work as educators in the broader sense,. Educaring from the heart invites us to consider our values-based approach and the spiritual influences shaping our work as educators across the continuum.

Perhaps the most important factor to consider in your identity as an educator is the motivation for your decision to become an educator. Why did you decide to become an educator? Was it a purposeful decision or an accidental journey? Are you content with your role and decision to work in education or are you uncertain about why you are here? Whatever your response to these questions, there is no doubt that education can be a really rewarding profession, with the privilege of witnessing and contributing directly to the growth of children and young people as they progress through the system. Equally, it can be the most challenging profession, with educators navigating the complex spaces between delivering curriculum and negotiating relational dynamics with children, young people and the wider educational community. It is especially challenging when trying to support children and young people in really difficult circumstances or when the passion or motivation to be there has dwindled or dimmed. There simply is nowhere to hide.

So why does our educator backpack matter? It matters because our educator identit(ies) shape who we are and how we approach the educational encounter. It reflects the complex intersection between our authentic and professional selves. Our educator backpacks matter because educators matter. Educators are the most influential factor impacting pupil and student learning and school effectiveness. Bringing awareness to who we are as educators is a critical aspect to reflective practice, which is increasingly promoted as a key contributor to the school improvement agenda. To ignore who we are as educators is to undermine the critical role our identities play in shaping the relational domain, which is the cornerstone of delivering curriculum and pedagogy in the classroom. Educators require time and space to engage in deeply reflective practice. This starts with comprehensive introspection into who we are as our authentic personal and professional selves, which helps us to understand all of the aspects we carry with us to the pedagogic encounter. Educaring from the heart is an invitation to shine a light into ourselves, to reflect on who we are as educators, and how that shapes our approach with pupils and students in the learning environment. It is the most powerful way to truly understand one of the most complex dynamics shaping teaching and learning in our education systems. This is an invitation to a journey of self-discovery as an educator, to better understand our critical work with our pupils and students in the classroom. The first step on this journey is to identify what it is you carry in your educator backpack (Figure 2.3).

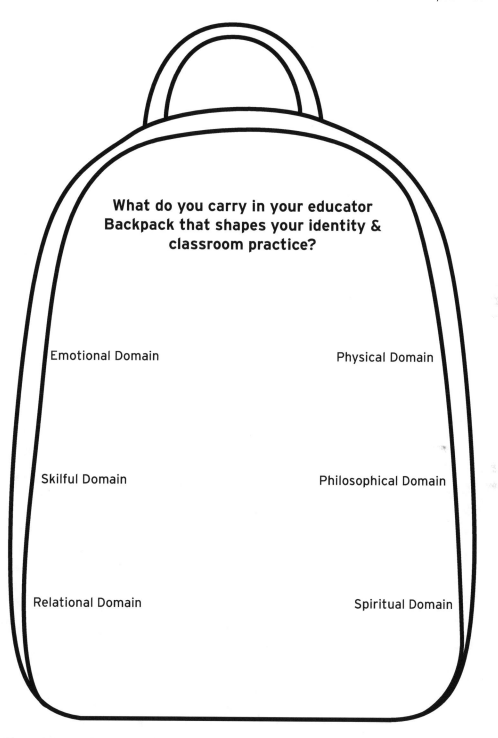

Figure 2.3 Exercise: Identifying the elements you carry in your educator backpack

References

Maslow, A. H. (1943). 'A theory of human motivation'. *Psychological Review*, 50(4), 370–396. https://doi.org/10.1037/h0054346

McIntosh, P. (1998). 'White privilege: Unpacking the invisible knapsack.' In M. McGoldrick (Ed.), *Re-visioning family therapy: Race, culture, and Gender in Clinical Practice*. Guilford Press.

Educaring from the Heart

Capture your thoughts & feelings here

3 Our Values

Our core values shape who we are as educators. They are deeply embedded within us, yet it is not often that we stop and reflect on how the values we hold as important in our personal lives, and as educators, influence our approach to the pedagogic encounter in the learning environment. Educaring from the heart requires us to be aware of our values, ensuring that they align with our authentic selves, embedding and framing them within an ethic of care, empathy, and compassion, and placing them at the core of our work with our students. Denying our values in and through our work as educators hinders our ability to engage in an authentic and genuine way with our pupils and students.

As we grow and evolve on our own life-course journeys, so too will our values. It is imperative that we take time out of the busyness of our lives to reflect on our values and how they are shaping our interaction with the world around us. Perhaps you are very clear on your values and how they are affecting your work as an educator. If this is true for you, use this chapter as an invitation to pause and reflect on whether your approach with your pupils/students aligns with your core personal and professional values. If, on the other hand, you have never explicitly considered or defined your values and would find them difficult to identify and name, use this chapter as an invitation to become aware of the core beliefs guiding you in your personal and professional life.

What are values? Educaring from the heart defines values as the deeply embedded and embodied beliefs influencing the ethical and moral compass of our lives. Our values are shaped by our life experiences, past and present, while also consciously or subconsciously determining our future behaviours and interactions. We can live much of our lives without being conscious of our values, operating in a passive mode, without considering how our beliefs and values shape our work as educators within a deeply relational and interdependent education system. Bringing greater attention and focus to our values and beliefs encourages us to reflect on the compass setting the course for our personal and professional journeys.

DOI: 10.4324/9781032718194-4

Awareness of our values can help us connect at a deeper level with our authentic selves, preparing us for more meaningful connections and relationships as educators, which will enhance the educational experience for everyone in the learning environment. Educaring from the heart invites us to re/evaluate our values, to hold them up for careful consideration and reflect on whether they are shaping how we interact and engage with the world in our everyday lives. Reflecting on our values helps us better understand ourselves and guides us in contributing to the positive emotional, psychological, and educational development of our pupils and students.

Our values are as unique and individual to us as our fingerprints. They are diverse and broad reaching, forming the lens through which we view and understand our lives and work as educators. While we may hold similar values to those around us, how we express those values through interactions in our lifeworld contexts is multifaceted and complex. Yet, when our values are at the heart of our work as educators, transformative possibilities arise for supporting and nurturing students to flourish and thrive within the education system and beyond. The power of one good adult in a young person's life is profound. It has the potential to empower pupils and students to transform their lives beyond what they can now imagine. However, the converse can sometimes also be true. While rare, an educator can negatively impact those around them by limiting the expectations and possibilities that pupils and students have for themselves both in education and beyond. Re/orienting and centering our authentic selves as educators around our values helps us become the type of "one good adult" we want to be in the lives of children and young people. Educaring from the heart can empower and transform our education system to be one that places care, empathy, and compassion at its core. Adopting such a values-based approach places educaring at its heart enabling effective teaching and learning.

Values are positive expressions of who we aspire and espouse to be in our daily lives. As such, values are an expression of our authentic selves. They provide us with a moral compass to guide our lives in a positive and lifegiving way. Values inform our perceptions of and interactions with those around us. They help us adopt a care-full, empathic, and compassionate approach to life, which is especially helpful for understanding the diverse perspectives of others around us. They are the firm foundation of educaring from the heart. Our values are shaped by our lived context, ethnic and cultural background, gender identity, socioeconomic circumstances, dis/ability, and sexual orientation, to name only a few. They also influence, and are influenced by, what we carry in our educator backpack.

Values are multifaceted, varied, and extremely personal to each educator. When educaring from the heart, it is important to (1) identify the values that are important to you and (2) consider how they are expressed in your work as an educator. In other words, how do your values inform your identity as your authentic self and how do they inform your identity as an educator? Are your individual values the same as those you espouse as an educator? Or do they differ? If they differ, how do they differ? And why do you think they differ?

The educaring from the heart definition of values offers a lens through which to better understand the role a values-embedded approach to education has for our practice in/though/with pedagogy in the learning environment (Figure 3.1).

For fear of stating the obvious, our values should be **values-based**. That is, they should be formulated around the values and beliefs we feel are important rather than the characteristics we believe we have. So how do values differ from characteristics? Characteristics are perceptions of how we think, feel, and behave. In contrast, values are deeply embedded and embodied ideas and beliefs that inform the decisions we make about our lives. Our values should be **actionable, dynamic**, and **responsive** as we practice them in our daily personal and professional lives. Values are **living**, ever evolving and constantly in flux, adapting and responding to our life context. Furthermore, our values are **unique** to who we are, reflecting our individuality and uniqueness in the world. Although we will share similar values with other individuals, how we understand and live out our values will be unique to our own life journeys. As such, our values are constantly **evolving**. Finally, our

Educaring from the heart - Values

Values based

Actionable

Living

Unique

Evolving

Soulful

Figure 3.1 Educaring from the heart - values

values should be **soulful**, resonating deeply with the innermost recesses of who we are as individuals and as educators.

Have you considered or reflected on your values? Educaring from the heart invites you to pause and reflect on your values to better understand your authentic self. Use the template in Figure 3.2 to represent the values you draw on to guide you on the decisions you make as you journey through your life.

What are your values as an educator? What values shape how you interact and engage with your pupils and students in your work as an educator? Is there any gap between the values you espouse and the values you actually realise through your work with students? This is an invitation to use the template in Figure 3.3 to reflect on your values as an educator.

Educaring from the heart encourages you to be more aware of your values you as an individual and as an educator working within and across the continuum of education. It is an invitation to reflect on any gaps that may emerge between your values and what you actually realise through the pedagogic encounter. When reviewing the two templates above, consider how your values converge/diverge from those you identify as important to your authentic self and those you espouse as an educator? Use the template in Figure 3.4 to help explore this is more depth.

While our values shape who we are and how we interact in the world, they are never fixed or unmalleable. They are constantly in flux, re/shaped, and re/formed through our life context. Education does not happen in a vacuum. The learning environment, and the nature of the relationships within, is shaped by several factors. These include the pupils and students in front of you at any given time; their needs, which are determined by the complexities of their lives; the culture of their educational institution; socioeconomic influences; relational dynamics; implicit and explicit expectations communicated to students and educators; the physical environment; leadership; policy initiatives; and external evaluation. Each of these factors directly affects how we realise our personal and professional values in and through our work with our pupils and students.

Educaring from the heart invites us to place care, empathy, and compassion at the core of our educational values as an anchor point for our pupils and students in and through the pedagogic encounter. It requires us to challenge any contextual factors that hinder the realisation of these values, and identify ways to address any barriers to the care, empathy, and compassion at the heart of our work. With these core values at the heart of educational institutions, all learners across the continuum from early childhood to higher and further education will have a more holistic and meaningful educational experience. Meaningful, effective learning only occurs when learners feel safe to take risks, be vulnerable, and fail without judgement. Cultivating the values of care, empathy, and compassion within and through our educational systems will nurture optimal conditions for children and young people to develop in a holistic way, ensuring they flourish and thrive in education and beyond.

Figure 3.2 Exercise: identify your life values

What values do you hold important as an educator?

Figure 3.3 Exercise: identify your educator values

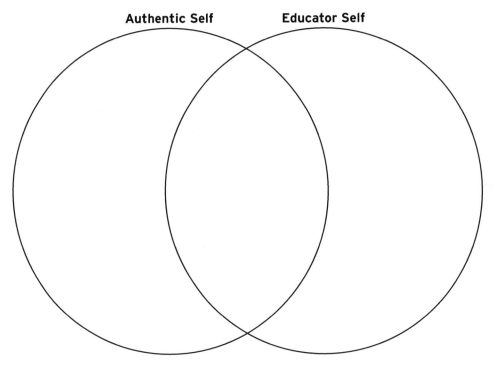

Convergent/Divergent Values

Authentic Self   **Educator Self**

Figure 3.4 Exercise: convergence & divergence of values

Educaring from the Heart

Capture your thoughts & feelings here

4 Our *Why*

Purpose. Have you ever taken a moment to reflect on your why? Why are you an educator? What path have you taken to this point in your professional life? How have you arrived here? Is this what you had planned and envisioned for your life? Does it fulfil you, give purpose and sustenance to your soul?

As educators, we are charged with helping those around us identify their gifts, talents, and passions, and to take tentative steps onwards in their life journeys. However, it is rare that educators have an opportunity to identify and remind ourselves of our purpose - our why. This why, or purpose in our life, provides us with a signpost to guide us in sharing our gift with the world. It provides the compass that steers us on our journey, keeping our ship on course, with a destination in clear view. Without a compass, a purpose, we can get lost, caught in a storm, without a clear understanding of why we are where we are and doing what we are doing. We get lost in the storm, destabilizing our ship and all onboard. Indeed, that lack of clear purpose can destabilize all aspects of our professional and personal lives, unable to see beyond the tsunami of waves overwhelming and confusing us. As we journey through our lives, our destination may change in response to what is going on around us. If this happens, it is important to intentionally set the destination, otherwise we may end up taking a path through a place we never chose to visit.

As we journey through our professional careers as educators we navigate and negotiate our way through lifecycles that can profoundly impact our work with pupils and students across the continuum of education. These educator lifecycles are shaped by our length of experience, the context of our work and its conditions, our career opportunities and professional development, and the demands of our personal life affect how much we can give of ourselves in our collective and individual roles. Often, we progress through these professional lifecycles unaware of how our journey is impacting on our purpose - that is, why we are working in education and doing what we are doing. The context of our work as educators can have a

DOI: 10.4324/9781032718194-5

profound impact on our stage in our career lifecycle, particularly when it comes to staying motivated and engaged within the profession.

So why, you may ask, is this important? Sometimes we can be carried through our educational careers without stopping to consider whether our purpose, our why, is fulfilling us and meeting our expectations. If we are not fulfilled in our work, how can we meet the needs of the learners in front of us in our classrooms? If we are stressed and unhappy, how can we support the emotional needs of our students? If we are unmotivated and disengaged, how can we be innovative, come alive in our teaching, and motivate our students? If we are not clear of our destination, our purpose, how can we be clear on our journey? As educators, our pupils and students accompany us on that journey through our work in the classroom. Knowing your why is as important as knowing who you are as an educator. It sets your intention for what it is you want to achieve in and through your work as educator. Purpose provides the sustenance to fuel our motivation. The educaring from the heart purpose model illustrates the interconnectedness between our why, our engagement, and our motivation as they are shaped and moulded by the context within which we work and live our lives (Figure 4.1).

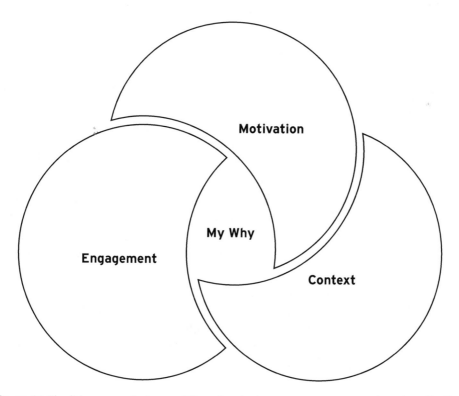

Figure 4.1 The interconnectedness of the educator's purpose, engagement, and motivation

We all have **a why**. This why is important to meet our vision for both our personal and professional lives. We all have a reason why we have taken a journey in education, whether intentionally or unintentionally. Have you taken time recently to stop and consider your why? Educaring from the heart is an invitation to take a moment to reflect on your purpose – why are you working in education? Perhaps your why has evolved and changed since you first entered education as a professional? Maybe you have lost your sense of why and are feeling unsure of where you are and where you want to be? Do you need to re/orientate your work to align more closely with your why? If so, what is it you need to do to align more closely with your overall purpose in education? This is an invitation to consider you why and re/discover your purpose in education (Figure 4.2).

Understanding our purpose is so important because it affects **our engagement** with and commitment to ourselves, to the educational profession, and to our pupils and students. If we are not clear on our purpose, we lose a sense of our professional identity, which influences how we understand ourselves as members of broader society. Our educational purpose guides the nature of our engagement in and across the profession. If we have a clear sense of our why, our intentional purpose, we are more likely to experience positive engagements with our colleagues and learners. Our why is expressed in our approach and practice in the learning environment, which also determines the nature of the pedagogic encounter. Together with our values, it underpins our work and engagement with our pupils/students and guides us in our educational journeys.

The purpose, or why, for many educators is focused around idealistic values of care, empathy, and compassion for children and young people. Indeed, this why is embedded within a desire to make a difference in the lives of those with whom we work. Having clarity on that aspect of our why directly impacts and shapes how we interact with and support the pupils and students in our classrooms. The power of positive engagement with children and young people cannot be underestimated in influencing positive outcomes for them in their educational experiences and life-course journeys. Your why can directly impact the life of a child and a young person through your engagement with them as an educator. Educaring from the heart is embedded within this ethic of care, which promotes positive engagement with children and young people placing them at the heart of what we do in the education system. This is an invitation to use the template in Figure 4.3 to consider your why as it relates to your work as an educator. It uses three key prompts: (1) How does your purpose influence your engagement as an educator? (2) What are the barriers to engaging in a heart-full way? and (3) What are the opportunities for you to overcome some of these barriers through the pedagogic encounter?

Clearly identifying your why not only contributes to the nature of your engagement as an educator, it also directly impacts on **your motivation**. A spiral effect

What is your why?

Figure 4.2 Exercise: Identifying your purpose in education

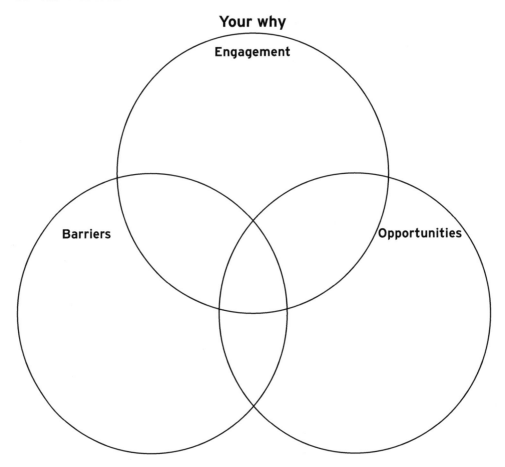

Figure 4.3 Exercise: Identifying the barriers and opportunities shaping your engagement
             as educator

emerges whereby having a clear understanding of your why results in your engagement and motivation continuously building upon each other, which further influences
your approach to educaring from the heart. Indeed, this relationship is symbiotic,
meaning that your engagement impacts your motivation. The more positive your
engagement, the greater your motivation; the greater your motivation, the more
positive your engagement. This is like the common psychological phenomenon of
action leading to motivation, which then results in action. In other words, to change
our thoughts and feelings, which drives our motivation, we need to take an action.

    While there are many forms of motivation, the two most dominant and spoken
about are intrinsic and extrinsic motivation. Extrinsic motivation is concerned with
the external factors and rewards that influence how we meet our goals as educators

in the classroom. This can include anything from engaging in continuing education and professional development to career progression and change. Intrinsic motivation is more personal and deeply connected to our why. Intrinsic motivation is the desire to do something or achieve a goal. In education, this could relate to your career satisfaction to the desire to make a difference in an individual's life. I invite you to use the template in Figure 4.4 to reflect on the factors motivating you and to remind yourself of your purpose as an educator.

Of course, the context within which we work re/defines our purpose as educators. The complex intersection of external factors, often beyond our control, affects who we are and the work we do as educators. Sometimes we can lose sight of our why in the midst of juggling the myriad contextual factors impacting us and our work. Educaring from the heart requires us to recognize these factors, which includes macroinfluences, the education system, institutional systems, and local community within which you work as an educator (Figure 4.5).

We should not underestimate the power of contextual factors to affect our purpose as educators. These factors directly impact our engagement with learners in and across our educational contexts. As such, they are extremely powerful considerations for how we understand ourselves as educators. **Macroinfluences** are especially important and often invisible when considering the flux and flow of educational policy and practice at the local level. International policymaking, like that of the Organisation for Economic Co-operation and Development (OECD), trickles down and influences policy and practice at local and individual educational systems. Such policies relate both to broader educational priorities, like re/defining educational purpose, as well as more focused directives, like teaching of numeracy, literacy, and wellbeing. Underpinning these international policy directives is a broader understanding of the purpose and value of education, which is often guided by a more neoliberal agenda of meeting economic and social needs at the global level. Furthermore, such global priorities directly inform national-level educational agendas, which are often responding to emerging needs and crises such as migration, climate change, and wellbeing.

The **education system** directly impacts how we experience our work as educators. Education systems are extremely complex. They are often re/shaped in response to stakeholder agendas and needs. As such, national policies and priorities are constantly in flux in response to competing demands across all levels – globally, societally, and communally. Education systems across the world vary due to the cultural influences re/shaping and re/defining them. These influences are embedded within the sociohistorical contexts from which our education systems emerged – that is, where our systems began and how they have grown and developed over time. Our cultural influences also shape, and are shaped by, the philosophical foundations of our education systems – that is, how we define the role and purpose

What motivates you as an educator?

Figure 4.4 Exercise: What motivates you as an educator?

Figure 4.5 Contextual Factors Influencing Educator Engagement

of education within and across our societies. The sociological and psychological bases of our education systems are especially important for educators and learners. The cultural influences on our systems play a role in determining how we define the socialization role of education in our societies. Partnership is critical in re/defining the role of education in re/shaping our citizens. For our education systems to be successful we need to have a common and shared understanding of their social purpose. Public engagement is especially important in this regard. Uninformed public opinion can result in divisive narratives that undermine and devalue our education systems, which is the foundation upon which our wider societies are built and re/formed.

Education systems around the world are typically comprised of institutions, the characteristics of which vary across its different levels. The **institutional systems** within which you work as an educator also re/shapes your why. Indeed, it may be that your work as an educator is defined by the institution within which you work, such as working in early childhood education settings or teaching at primary/elementary, secondary/high school, or college/further education/university level. Our pedagogical practices, which are informed by national policy, are also formed by the institutional systems within which we work. There is, arguably, little opportunity for crosspollination of these practices across the education continuum. The institutional systems within which we work can establish the nature of our purpose and our why, as we work to re/define our roles in education. For example, while working at primary/elementary level can be perceived as very different from higher or further education, many pedagogies and approaches can be applied across the continuum to enrich the educators' work and their respective learning environments. This lost opportunity is often overlooked in education.

The curricular content and assessment procedures play an important role in our work at all educational levels. Education systems embedded within neoliberal societies are inherently competitive. Assessment is used as a tool for measuring learning and performance outcomes for pupils and students – and educators too, by proxy. The nature of our why as educators also arises from the professional development and career opportunities that mark our professional life journeys. One of the often-mentioned limitations within education is the minimal career opportunities for upward and lateral movement within educational institutions. This can result in disengagement and loss of motivation for educators. Effective, high quality, and dynamic professional learning opportunities can enhance motivation, reinvigorating educators as they return to their classrooms with new methodologies or perspectives on their professional purpose. Such positive experiences can result in educators reflecting on and reviewing their why, motivating them to perhaps re/orientate their purpose in the education system.

The **community** within which we work as educators has a profound impact on our purpose and our why. Our contexts are so multifaceted and diverse that no two environments can ever be considered the same. Indeed, the heterogeneity of the education system is the result of its dynamic responsiveness to changes within our societies. This can positively contribute to our work as educators, yet it can also be overwhelming when change happens suddenly with little time to plan and/or respond. The speed of change within our education systems and communities is profound. The intensification of its demands, especially on our time, puts immense pressure on educators around the globe. It is questionable whether this acceleration of education has any benefit for students, educators, educational institutions, their communities, or our societies more broadly. Perhaps it reflects an undercurrent within our modern world that promotes the risk of being overwhelmed and left behind. Perhaps we should consider slowing down education, as a matter of urgency, so we can re/define our greater purpose and vision for education's place in our wider societies. Our children and young people deserve nothing less. Indeed, it is no coincidence that we are witnessing an increase in anxiety among children and young people in our education system.

Our work as educators is informed by the community with which we interact and work. Children and young people constitute the main body of our educational community. They bring with them diversity of gender, social class, ethnicity, and dis/ability. As such, the needs of students in our classrooms have a profound impact on our why. As educational research and psychological assessment availability improves, the diverse needs of our students are increasingly identified, resulting in a greater demand on resources to support pupils and students in their learning. The absence or scarcity of resources to meet these needs or to implement the needed changes to pedagogic practice can be frustrating and challenging to navigate. Indeed, performativity measures, when used as cold metrics to measure school and educational effectiveness, can also affect how educators engage with their students. The socioeconomic position of the community within which a school is located can also impact educators. Supporting students and their families as they navigate the complexities of poverty requires that educators be empathic, compassionate, and responsive to their needs. This can be especially challenging in communities of socioeconomic disadvantage where needs can be diverse and more complex.

Navigating classroom dynamics can be especially challenging in classrooms where students have diverse and complex socioemotional needs. Classroom teaching can be a like a pressure cooker at times, simmering on the brink of explosion. This can be really challenging for educators who must respond in a compassionate and empathetic manner. Many educators refer to classroom volatility as 'firefighting' when they must respond to students who, through no fault of their own, express their trauma and distress in behaviours that can be perceived as verbal, and even physical, abuse. While such behaviours are not the norm, it is certainly an aspect of working in education that directly affects an educator's purpose and vision. Conversely, working with students and seeing them flourish and thrive in education and beyond fills the pale for our work as educators. Indeed, the power of one cannot be underestimated. While, as educators, we aspire to have a positive impact on all students, this is not always possible or realistic. Educaring from the heart is about meeting all students with care, empathy, and compassion to support them in challenging circumstances, but also finding the value of making a positive difference to an individual's life.

One of the greatest factors affecting educators' engagement and motivation is the institutional culture within which they work. Leadership is crucial to nurturing an environment where educators can flourish, realise their purpose, and thrive in education. Professional trust, which means being valued and encouraged to take risks within a learning environment, is especially important for an educator's agency and sense of belonging in an educational institution. If we, as educators, are afforded the professional freedom to realise our own purpose, this will encourage more meaningful engagement and motivation in our work. Indeed, it will empower us to lead more fulfilling careers, far surpassing the expectations and limitations of effective teaching and learning that are set by our institutional cultures. Educaring from the heart requires school leadership to create a culture that empowers educators to realise their vision and purpose by taking risks and being creative and innovative in the pedagogic encounter. Valuing the work of educators serves to enhance pupil/student experiences and learning. Educaring from the heart begins with caring for the communities within which our educational institutions are embedded.

The exercise in Figure 4.6 is an invitation to reflect on the contextual factors affecting your why at the moment? Is there anything you can do to help you overcome or embrace these factors to better understand how they are re/shaping your understanding of your vision or your why?

So how does this relate to educaring from the heart? To have clarity on the factors bearing upon and re/shaping your vision and your why, it is important to understand the contextual factors informing your experiences within the education system. In the absence of such understanding, we can lose our way, becoming disorientated and unclear why we are doing what we are doing. This can result in feelings of disillusionment. Educaring from the heart calls on us to awaken our awareness and identify what may be holding us back from realising our vision and purpose as an educator. It calls on us to dig deep and to free the shackles of what may be holding us back from realizing our vision and purpose as an educator. It starts by identifying the factors influencing our work, both in positive and challenging ways. From there, we can create a road map for harnessing the positive influences and reorientating ourselves around the challenges to ensure we are meeting our vision and purpose as educators. When the system fails to support us in realizing our professional purposes and desires, they are also failing our pupils/students. Educaring from the heart invites us to have these critical conversations, to nurture and cultivate the positive while challenging the barriers preventing us from realizing our vision, our why, which drives our engagement and motivation in and through our work.

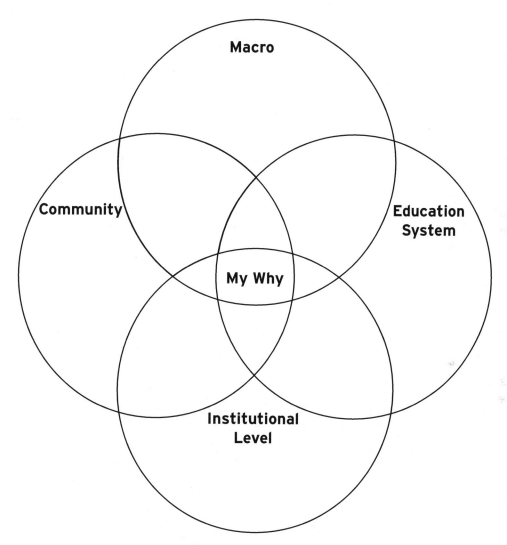

Figure 4.6 Exercise: Identifying contextual factors impacting your engagement as an educator

Educaring from the Heart

Capture your thoughts & feelings here

5 Our Wellbeing

Increasingly, we live in an arguably increasingly toxic culture where hurry and haste holds higher value and status than slowing down and taking our time. Busyness is considered an acceptable and even expected status within contemporary society. This is reflected in many of the structures dominating and influencing how we live our lives, including education. There is always something to do, and never enough time to do it. The surveillance of how we use our time further compounds the fear and anxiety that we are not making full use of our time, particularly in education. What ensues is a perfect storm, where time becomes a resource rather than an expectation, a luxury rather necessity, resulting in chronic intensification of time that affects both physical health and mental wellbeing. Contemporary neoliberal agendas dictate how we experience time and space. These agendas are underpinned by the capitalist idea that *time is money*. The resulting cost is our collective health and wellbeing. We find ourselves grappling with trying to make sense of our time-pressured lives, feeling under increasing pressure, which manifests as stress and a negative sense of wellbeing. As a result, we seek relief through four different psychological responses: fight, flight, fawn, or freeze (Table 5.1).

Within education, you may experience a fight response, leading to conflict with others, because of the overwhelming demands made of your time. This can be challenging for nurturing and maintaining positive working relationships in educational institutions. Flight is experienced as seeking to escape a situation, either a short-term timeout from your working environment or a decision to exit the profession. Indeed, increasing attrition rates across the continuum of education are concerning, particularly when considering the valuable role educators play in re/forming and re/shaping our societies. The retention of high quality educators in our education systems is a key to ensuring we have healthy and well-adjusted societies, according to all measures (such as wellbeing, economic, social, and inclusion). Fawning is seeking to please those around you to deal with overwhelming feelings. Freezing results from feeling disempowered, stuck, and unable to find a response to the threat you

DOI: 10.4324/9781032718194-6

Table 5.1 Trauma Responses

Four Types of Trauma Responses	
Fight	Responding to a threat in an aggressive manner
Flight	Running from a threat
Fawn	Avoiding conflict by pleasing others
Freeze	Not moving or acting against a threat

are experiencing in your working life. Our responses to the complexities of change that occur in our lives, both at a personal and professional level, are natural and normal. While the reasons evoking such responses ought to be problematized, we should normalize and accept our responses for the normal and natural stress reactions to challenging circumstances they are.

Seeking and finding relief from the pressures of our daily lives is challenging. Our working lives play a crucial role in our experience of time, space, and place, directly impacting our health and wellbeing. Indeed, many of the mental health agendas of our workplaces were introduced in response to international policies stressing the importance of wellbeing in work environments. While such policies support individual wellbeing, they also serve to paper over the cracks, or rather the deep chasm, at the core of the issue. We expect more of people and give them less time to achieve it. Our human response to this situation is natural - stress and a corresponding trauma. However, stress in itself is not the issue. It is merely the symptom of a chronic dis/ease deeply impacting our societies - the intensification of time.

Education is the cornerstone of our society. As an ideal, education strives for the holistic development of the child/young person, shaping how they understand themselves and others as citizens of the world. However, this ideal is often in conflict with the reality of our educational institutions. The embodied experience of education is as important as the messages communicated, directly and indirectly, by our institutions. Those messages are referred to as the explicit and hidden curriculum. The direct conflict between the messages communicated in/through education institutions and the individual's educational experiences can confuse, disorientate, and make them uncertain, undermining the individual, our institutions, and ultimately our societies. For example, how we experience the practices of wellbeing and mental health in education can be in direct contradiction to the messages emphasising its importance that we are given. This can confuse educators and students alike, as these messages are in direct conflict to the lack of time for wellbeing practices in education. The confusion and disorientation that follows leads to self-blame for not doing enough or for doing something wrong, particularly when accompanied by a decline in mental health and wellbeing. This represents the pinnacle of power within the system, when the individual turns a systemic failure inward, blaming themselves for experiencing stress, a natural response to the chronic intensification of time. This results in a sense of powerlessness, uncertainty, and confusion. Such disorientation works in favour of a system that claims to support your wellbeing while at the same time creating the conditions, through policies and practices, that actively and directly contribute to declining mental health across our educational institutions.

So, do we give up and accept that this is how it is now in education? Doing so would be a travesty. Educators have more power than they believe. In a world where the pressures on our education systems to solve many social issues, educaring from the heart is a countercultural approach that advocates for educators to stop and care for themselves and for their students first. It is a call to reject and rebuff the demands made of educator time that come at the cost of our individual and collective wellbeing. As educators, we have the privileged position of directly influencing and shaping our students' understanding and experience of education. Educators are the most influential factor in educational effectiveness and improvement. As such, our individual efforts can have a profound impact on collective experiences. Educaring from the heart is a call to action, to empower educators to embrace their agency in nurturing their individual wellbeing, as well as that of their pupils/students, as a countercultural action in response to the hurry and haste we are currently experiencing within and across our education systems. It is an invitation to a microaction that can have a profound impact on our macrosystems, including our broader societies. We often underestimate the power of one person to make significant impact on the lives of those in our educational institutions.

Wellbeing in education has garnered increased attention over the past few years, often solely focusing on the pupil/student. However, less attention is given to the wellbeing of educators within the system. In instances where educator wellbeing is referred to in policy, it is often perceived as tokenistic rather than meaningful. Such perceptions are not unsurprising given the increasingly demanding expectations placed on educators working across the continuum. Education is often perceived as fertile ground to address wider societal issues and challenges, an expectation to introduce and implement initiatives to respond to critical issues within our societies. As a result, educational institutions can experience initiative overload. Such initiatives are often introduced as add-ons on to the requirements of an already intensive curriculum. Furthermore, in instances where there is curriculum change, the demands made of educators can be especially challenging to implement in the classroom. As research into and greater understanding of neurodiversity emerges and evolves, the complexities of meeting learners' needs also deepens. Educaring from the heart means ensuring that every child or young person is valued, respected, and accepted for who they are in the classroom. Such work is crucial and valued by educators, while also demanding skills, expertise, and time to ensure the needs of all pupils/students are met in education. Educators often find themselves task burdened and time poor. The de/valuing and eroding of time in education is especially concerning. We cannot expect educators to meet the demands made of them if we do not provide them with the time and means to do so.

It is no surprise that the competing demands made of educators has a profound impact on their wellbeing. I call this our relational wellbeing. An educator's wellbeing has a direct impact on the nurturing and negotiation of relationships in the learning environment. As a result, the wellbeing of educators is absolutely critical to ensure we are nurturing positive relationships while also contributing to the positive holistic development of our pupils/students across our education system. Relational wellbeing is very much determined by how we experience time, space, and place within and across the education system (Figure 5.1).

Relational wellbeing is the ability for both educators and pupils/students to relate and interact in a positive way that enhances their wellbeing. Relational wellbeing is a key element and outcome of educaring from the heart. It is symbiotic in nature. Positive wellbeing ensures positive interactions, while those positive

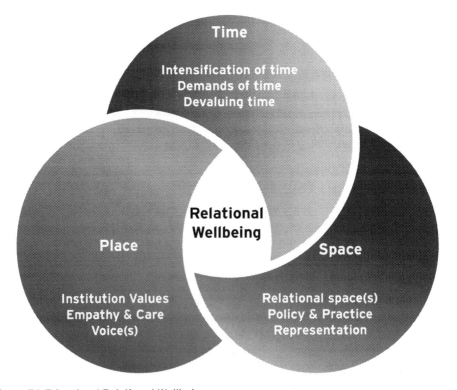

Figure 5.1 Educators' Relational Wellbeing

interactions enhance both the wellbeing of educator and pupil/student. Time, space, and place play an important role in contributing to positive relational wellbeing.

Time structures the way educators and children/young people experience their lives in education. It dictates the rhythm of our days and weeks as determined by and experienced across our educational institutions. Time provides both opportunities and limitations to curriculum delivery and the pedagogic encounter. Time shapes the re/construction of social worlds in education, influencing how and when educators, pupils/students, and the wider school community interact and relate. The regulation and surveillance of time within education can contribute to a limiting of possibilities to engage in more creative and innovative approaches in teaching and learning. Over the past decade we have witnessed an **intensification of time** in education, with the demands on both educator and pupil/student time ever increasing. This is especially evident in the increasing demand for accountability and evaluation, which places pressure on educators to provide evidence and a measurable accounting of their time. We have witnessed the emergence of a productivity paradox in which educators are expected to increase productivity within the limits of the existing time available to them. This shrinking of time means that educators are more often expected to do more with the time they have. This includes curricular reform, adopting new initiatives and approaches, engaging with digital technologies, meeting the increasingly complex needs of learners/students, and adopting a universal design approach for learning. Educators respond to these demands by engaging in continuous professional development, often undertaking courses or programmes of study outside of working hours, placing increasing pressure on their personal time. This intensification of time in education places greater **demands of time** on educators in the absence of providing them with the most important resource they need to realise the increased workload – time. Educator and pupil/student wellbeing is negatively impacted by the ever-increasing workload and the ensuing intensification of time. This is evident in increasing anxiety and burnout across our education systems. While policies have been specifically introduced to enhance wellbeing, they are targeted at addressing the symptoms, and do very little to address the core of the problem, which is increasing demands and time pressure on everyone across our educational communities. As a result, we are witnessing a **devaluing of time** in education. We are at a critical moment within our education system, requiring us to critically reflect on how we de/value and prioritise time. Time, as a construct in education, serves to regulate and determine how individuals experience their daily lives, including teaching, learning, and social interactions. The de/valuing of time within education threatens to erode the work of educaring from the heart – providing quality time to put care, empathy, and compassion at the core of work and approaches to teaching and learning through the pedagogic encounter. This has particularly profound implications for relational wellbeing in education. De/valuing time threatens to erode the opportunities and possibilities for positive relational interactions within the classroom, negatively affecting relational wellbeing within education.

Space plays a critical role in supporting positive relational wellbeing in education. Space is the physical environment within which wellbeing can be positively cultivated and nurtured. Creating the most optimal physical space and environment for positive wellbeing to flourish and thrive is especially important. The provision of **relational space(s)** provides optimal conditions for growing and nurturing positive relationships, where educators, pupils/students and the wider school community can come together in a safe environment to explore and understand who they are as citizens in the world. The way we allocate and use space in education is determined by **policy and practice**. Competing demands, driven by policy directives within education, places pressure on and determines decisions about how space is used and valued within settings. Such decisions directly impact the educator's and pupil's/student's experience of relational wellbeing as it is influenced by the opportunities and nature of interactions within an educational setting. High quality relational spaces contribute to more positive relational wellbeing. It is critical to ensure that educational policy and practice provide for relational spaces where all members of an educational community can come together to engage in a meaningful way to nurture their wellbeing. **Representation** is essential to ensuring that all members within the educational community are meaningfully represented within an educational setting, and across our education systems more broadly. Space plays a vital role in ensuring representation by providing the physical environment within which all members of our society are equally represented and visible within and across our education systems. Representation cultivates a sense of belonging, valuing, and accepting, which enhances the nature of relationships and contributes to positive wellbeing. Educaring from the heart calls on education systems and institutions to consider the critical role that space plays in cultivating positive relational wellbeing in education, placing emphasis on care, empathy, and compassion in policy and practice, determining how physical space is used and valued.

Place determines how space is used within education, which influences relational wellbeing. The physical spaces within which educators and students experience relational wellbeing are located within places across our education system. **Institutional values** determine the nature of teaching and learning within educational places, shaping how educators and pupils/students interact and negotiate their learning environments. Values are shaped by the level at which the institution operates (that is, from early childhood education to higher and further education), as well as by the characteristics of the children/young people with whom they are interacting. Institutional values signpost and prioritise principles that are considered to be at the core of their work, ultimately determining the nature of the teaching and learning experience in the classroom. The institutional values espoused by places for education across our system ultimately determine how our children and young people experience **empathy and care**. Places determine the policies and practices employed within educational spaces. Educaring from the heart calls for places in education to situate care, empathy, and compassion at the core of their values, policies, and practices to nurture positive relational wellbeing. Place holds power and potential for **voice(s)** in education. The places and institutions across our education systems play a critical role in contributing to the development of our understanding of the meaning of citizenship – including global citizenships – within our particular societies. A key aspect of citizenship is voice. Ensuring that places for education value voice(s), which means providing time, space, and due consideration to the opinions of all members, is especially important for nurturing relational wellbeing. To have voice is to be empowered. It is incumbent that all educational institutions provide opportunities for their communities to share their voice(s), to give such contributions due consideration, and to act upon the opinions that are shared. This is especially important for those most marginalized within our educations system, across the continuum. It is our ethical and moral responsibility to ensure that all voice(s) are included in how we define and value education as a societal purpose. It is also critical to ensure the voice(s) of children and young people are placed at the heart of our discussions about education. Educaring from the heart starts with those at the heart of our education system – our children and young people from all social backgrounds and giving due consideration to gender, race, ethnicity, social class, and dis/ability.

Educators are also at the heart of our education system, occupying one of the most important and influential spaces. We cannot expect to have healthy and thriving education systems if we actively ignore educator wellbeing. As discussed in this chapter, the complexities of our education system and the multiplicity of competing demands and agendas have profound impact on individual and collective wellbeing within education, and especially for educators. It is important to recognize that, although we are working as educators within an increasingly intensified education system, we also have agency to contribute to and nurture our individual and collective wellbeing. The next section of this chapter seeks to guide and support you in identifying opportunities and practices to take control over and support your wellbeing in education.

One of the most empowering ways to take control of your wellbeing is to identify and name the "what." What are the factors that are impacting your wellbeing? How are they affecting your wellbeing (positively/negatively)? Identifying and naming the "what" offers the possibility of taking the unknown and bringing it into the light, empowering you to identify what you can control and perhaps change, and, equally, what you have little or no control and perhaps can let go (Figure 5.2).

What factors in education are impacting on your wellbeing?

Factor	Positive or Negative Impact	Controllable or Non-Controllable

Figure 5.2 Exercise: Identify factors that impact your wellbeing in education

This next template (Figure 5.3) is an invitation to consider the factors you have named in the previous exercise to identify the factors impacting your wellbeing you can let go off (marked by the seed blowing away), and those you can address through your thinking and approach to your work as an educator (marked by the seed attached to the stem).

Decision making is a critical to nurturing your wellbeing. The first step may be to acknowledge that your wellbeing needs attention. In fact, wellbeing is akin to the heart. The more you exercise to strengthen your heart (a muscle), the stronger your heart becomes. This is also true for our wellbeing. Taking small steps and implementing sustainable practices in our lives can enhance or strengthen our wellbeing. However, your heart may be critically ill and need intervention or medical support before you can exercise to make it stronger. This is true of our mental wellbeing too. If you are in an overwhelming situation, are mentally exhausted, and the darkness is weighing heavy on you, this may be an indication that you need an intervention. Start by reaching out to your doctor or medical practitioner for help. You can also find support from local mental health organisations and occupational health (if available to you).

It is also important to acknowledge that mental wellbeing is never linear. It is never a straightforward, upward enhancement in our mental wellbeing. Drawing on the analogy of the heart, our mental wellbeing is like a heart rate throughout the day. It wavers from very low to very high, especially as it is strengthened and enhanced through exercise. The same is true for mental wellbeing. It is normal to have good periods where we experience positive wellbeing, followed by challenging periods where we feel low. It is important that when we hit those lows we do not remain there. We need to identify wellbeing practices to support us as individuals, enhancing our wellbeing and carrying us through those more challenging periods. Everyone is unique and this will be reflected in the wellbeing strategies that work for them. No two wellbeing action plans will ever be the same.

"The Five Ways to Wellbeing" framework developed by the New Economics Foundation has provided a useful evidence-based approach to supporting and enhancing positive mental health in populations across the globe (Aked, J., Marks, N., Cordon, C. and Thompson, S. (2008)). The five ways are connect, be active, take notice, keep learning, and give. These five ways of wellbeing are explored and considered as applicable in educational contexts. Educaring from the heart has included a sixth specifically relevant to educators working within temporally, emotionally, psychologically and physically intensive learning environments - step back and step out. These six pillars of educator wellbeing will now be discussed (Figure 5.4).

The first pillar of positive mental wellbeing is *connect*. Working as an educator can be a lonely and, at times, isolating role. While connecting may seem like a bizarre suggestion, given that those working in education are around people all day,

The Dandelion Exercise

What can you let go of?

What can you address?

Figure 5.3 Exercise: The Dandelion

6 Pillars for Educator Wellbeing

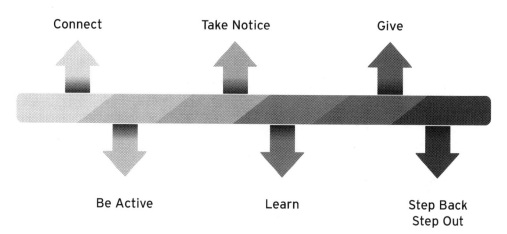

Figure 5.4 The six pillars of educator wellbeing

the workload and worries of an educator can result in feelings of isolation and lone-liness at times. Educaring from the heart encourages educators to connect with others, share authentic experiences, and recognize that others carry similar work-loads and worries. This can bring with it a sense of liberation and freedom rather than isolated struggle. Communities of practice play a important role in bringing educators together to cultivate circles of support and connection in and through education.

The second pillar of wellbeing in education is *be active*. Educators often live intellectually, in our heads, planning, reflecting, evaluating, considering, wor-rying, caring, wondering and so on. We can sometimes be very detached from our physical bodies and needs. Being active stimulates our feel-good hormones and is an important aspect of holistic wellbeing. This is especially important for ensuring we bring awareness to our physical selves, as well as our intellectual/emotional/psychological selves. Educaring is a physical undertaking and as such, it is important we express our wellbeing in and through our bodies and being active is an effective way of doing so.

The next pillar of educator wellbeing calls on us to *take notice*, to be present and aware of our self within our surroundings. This can be particularly challenging in the intensive educational environment where the needs of others take priority over our own. Making time to take notice in the busyness of our days is especially impor-tant for nurturing our wellbeing. In times of crises or extreme stress, taking notice is crucial for gauging the emotional temperature of the learning environment and in managing the moment-to-moment flux and flow of relational dynamics.

The fourth pillar for educator wellbeing calls for us to *keep learning*. As educators, we are experts at learning, with the majority of us engaging in lifelong learning on our professional journeys. Many of us are passionate about learning. However, it is equally important, in order to nurture our souls and our mental wellbeing, to learn something outside our profession, which can take us out of our heads again and into the joy and fun of learning. It provides us with insights into the journey of a learner negotiating something new or exciting within our own learning environments.

The fifth pillar of educator wellbeing encourages us to *give*. While this may be counterintuitive since we give so much of ourselves in our work as educators, finding ways to contribute to our communities outside of the educational environment can also enhance our mental wellbeing. We should consider opportunities to transfer our skills and talents to other areas within our communities to contribute positively to the lives of those around us. It is through giving that we grow.

The sixth pillar of educator wellbeing, a core aspect of educaring from the heart, is to step back and step out. This pillar is specifically important for educators negotiating the busyness of their professional lives. Moments of challenge or crisis can occur within the educational environment. Within these moments, educators are put under particularly intense pressure to ensure they respond in an appropriate and compassionate way. All too often educators are expected to pick up and continue regardless of the challenges and crises they meet within the educational environment. This pillar invites educators to step back from these moments or circumstances and step out of the situation, marked by the busyness of their professional and personal lives, and make time for the silence and solitude to reflect and just be. These moments are rare within education but they have never been more necessary for supporting and nurturing positive mental wellbeing among educators.

Educaring from the heart is an invitation to bring awareness to these 6 pillars to wellbeing, to identify those requiring more attention in your professional and personal lives and to consider the suggested tools as a means for meeting your needs in supporting your wellbeing as an educator. Table 5.2 provides a list of tools that may help in identifying practices and approaches to meet your wellbeing needs, as well as prompts to guide you in identifying an appropriate tool or practice to support your own unique needs.

Educaring from the heart also invites you to develop a personalised action plan for supporting and enhancing your wellbeing as an educator in both your personal and professional life. Use the template below (Figure 5.5) to design your wellbeing action plan. Make sure to choose tools or activities that you can incorporate into your already busy life. It may be that you choose to start with one practice and build in additional tools, as each practice becomes a habit in your life.

Table 5.2 Exercise: Identifying practices for supporting educator wellbeing

Six pillars of Educator Wellbeing	Tools and Practices for Educators	Prompt
Connect	Connect with those in your life Connect with likeminded educators Make new connections Connect with yourself Join a club/professional network	What opportunities are there to connect with others? Are there additional opportunities to make connections? Who is important in your life and when and how can you connect with them? Is there an opportunity to make new connections?
Be active	Exercise Walk Move your body to activate the parasympathetic nervous system Incorporate movement into pedagogy	How can you increase activity in your daily life? What supports your activity? When is the best time to be active in your daily life?
Take notice	Breathing exercises Mindfulness Journalling Mindful walking Gratitude Quality sleep Spend time in nature Mindful activities (jigsaw puzzles, Lego, diamond painting, etc.)	What are you doing in the moment? Are you being present and taking notice of your environment? Are you in your head or in your body? What tools/practices support you to be present in the moment?
Keep learning	Take up a new hobby Tap into your creativity Play /listen to music Engage in professional learning Learn outside of education	Is there something new you want to learn? How can you learn something new? When could you do so?
Give	Volunteer for something new Reach out and contribute to your local community (outside of education)	Is there an opportunity to give to others in your life? What ways would you enjoy giving to others? What times and means can you identify for giving to others?
Step back & step out	Take a timeout Step back rather than reacting immediately Spend time with yourself in silence	How can you step back from the moment and out of the busyness? When can you spend time with yourself in silence? Where can you retreat when the day is demanding? How can you step back from the intensity and busyness?

Wellbeing Action Plan

| Small steps to wellbeing | Tools to enable small steps | Making time for small steps |

Figure 5.5 Exercise: Educator wellbeing action plan

Wellbeing Action Plan Review

What is working well?	What is not working well?	Changes to make

Figure 5.6 Exercise: Educator wellbeing action plan review

Consider your wellbeing action plan as a living document, never fixed, always responsive to your needs as they change, develop, and evolve. Review your wellbeing action plan on a regular basis to assess whether it is working for you in a meaningful way (Figure 5.6). Taking time to do so will refocus your attention on yourself, your wellbeing, and the small steps you can take to nurture your wellbeing as an educator. Caring for your wellbeing is crucial to ensure you can educare from your heart and support the wellbeing of pupils/students in your learning environment.

Caring for your wellbeing as an educator has never been so important. The first steps require setting an intention, taking an action, and putting them into practice. It is only through intentionality and practice that small changes can become embedded within the day-to-day actions of our lives. Being consistent with our practice contributes directly to forming a habit and an expectation around behaviours that nurture positive wellbeing. Educaring from the heart is an invitation to take one small step forward on a journey to wellbeing that may just change your life on a personal and professional level.

References

Aked, J., Marks, N., Cordon, C. and Thompson, S. (2008), "Five Ways to Wellbeing: a report presented to the Foresight Project on communicating the evidence base for improving people's wellbeing", available at: https://neweconomics.org/uploads/files/five-ways-to-wellbeing-1.pdf (accessed 08 May 2024).

Educaring from the Heart

Capture your thoughts & feelings here

Part 2: The "Us" as Educator and Student

6 Nurturing the Individual

Nurturing the individual pupil/student so they can flourish and thrive in our education system is at the fulcrum of educaring from the heart. As discussed in the previous chapter, this can only truly be realized to its fullness once we nurture and support educator wellbeing across the education system. Indeed, education is coming together in community. This starts with the meeting between two individuals in particular, the educator and the pupil/student. Placing the student, child, young person, or other individual at the heart of the education system is core to re/orientating the values we espouse, the purposes we seek to realise, and the approaches we take to and through the pedagogic encounter. Educaring from the heart places the individual pupil/student at the heart of our education system.

Earlier in this book, I invited educators to identify their why or purpose for working in education. However, it is not often we can consider and reflect upon the purpose we espouse for our education system. What is it we wish to achieve in and through our education system? What is the purpose of the work we do as educators in our respective educational settings, as well as in the education system more broadly? What values are underpinning our education system? Do they support or hinder the realisation of the greater purpose we aim to achieve? How does this vision for education within our institutions and within our regions impact the work we do in our educational settings with pupils/students/children/young people? It is crucially important to reflect on this as educators because such values, visions, and purposes in education directly influence (a) the work we do, (b) the environments and cultures within which we work, and (c) the pedagogic approaches we employ.

Education is a collective action that begins with the individual, hence the importance of placing the individual at the heart of the work we do as educators. Our role as educators is to meet the individual where they are, identifying their strengths and needs, and making a plan to bring that student on a journey of learning. It is incumbent upon educators to nurture the individual, to support them in their journey, to enable them to flourish, thrive, and realise their fullest potential both

DOI: 10.4324/9781032718194-8

in education and beyond. Educaring from the heart begins with the meeting and opening of hearts.

Vulnerability and risk are at the heart of this process. Both educators and pupils/ students must take a risk, embrace vulnerability to engage with each other in an authentic and open way. Psychological safety is important in creating an environment wherein pupils/students can be their authentic selves, which is the foundation upon which they can meaningfully flourish and thrive within education. Educators must be skilled in creating the conditions for pupils/students to feel supported enough to truly be themselves. Only when children and young people can truly be themselves can they authentically learn and grow within the education system. Educaring from the heart calls on educators to cocreate learning environments where risk taking, vulnerability, and psychological safety are valued and nurtured (Figure 6.1).

Vulnerability is a core aspect of an educator's work. It is often overlooked as an important aspect of meaningful engagement and effective teaching. Effective teaching is realized in and through vulnerability. As educators, we are vulnerable when we open ourselves emotionally, psychologically, intellectually, and physically to engagement in the very public space of the learning environment. The act of teaching is one of vulnerability. We open ourselves up in front of a group

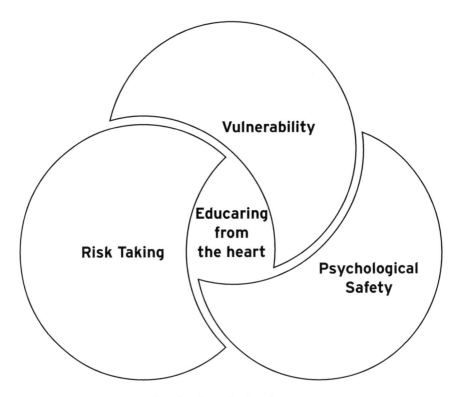

Figure 6.1 Characteristics of educaring from the heart

of individuals (pupils/students) to nurture and support them in their educational and psychosocial development. Equally, we expect our learners to engage, becoming vulnerable too in these public spaces, which are commonly occupied by the wider educational community and their peers. Indeed, being vulnerable in front of peers is one of the most challenging aspects for both learners and educators alike. It takes much courage to be vulnerable in and through the pedagogic encounter. If vulnerability is rejected or rebuked, even in a minor way, it can hinder the possibility for pupils/students and educators to re/engage in vulnerable exchanges in their educational journeys. To be vulnerable takes great courage from all members of the learning community. Being vulnerable in education is a decision. That decision determines the nature of the engagement between educator and pupil/student, which is affected by the degree of vulnerability expressed at any particular moment in time. It also determines the ability of educator to nurture and support pupil/student academic and social development. Educaring from the heart requires vulnerability from both educator and learner to engage in a meaningful and authentic way through the pedagogic encounter.

Psychological safety is especially important in creating the optimal conditions within which educators and pupils/students can be vulnerable in the classroom. While it is the role/responsibility of the educator to hold space for psychological safety in the classroom, it is also important for the learner to exercise their own agency in contributing to an environment in which all learners can experience psychological safety, be vulnerable, and engage in authentic and meaningful learning experiences. Creating a learning environment within which educators and students feel psychologically supported can be challenging given the complex dynamics of interacting in the classroom. This includes influences such as school culture, leadership, relationships (including those between educator and pupil/student, and between pupils/students themselves), curricular content, and pedagogical practices. Meaningful teaching and learning can only begin when both educators and pupils/students feel psychologically safe. While safety begins with the physical environment, including the context within which a learning environment is located, creating psychologically safe learning environments can be more complex because they are re/shaped and re/defined by the complex interactions constantly in flux between and within the physical spaces of the classroom. The educator is constantly re/negotiating such dynamic interactions to ensure that pupils/students can engage in effective learning in a safe space. Holding psychologically safe spaces for learners requires masterful educator skills to respond in a dynamic and reflexive way to challenges as they arise, moment to moment. Educaring from the heart requires that learning spaces support psychological safety, enabling learners to engage in a vulnerable way in and through their learning experiences.

Creating and nurturing a psychologically safe learning environment demands awareness and skill from the educator to ensure that pupils/students (and indeed educators themselves) are comfortable and open to learning within the most opti-mal of learning environments. The key characteristics of the psychologically safe learning environment when educaring from the heart are presented in Figure 6.2.

Arguably, the most important aspect of creating and nurturing a psycholog-ically safe learning environment is **trust**. Trust ensures that both students and educators can be vulnerable, take risks and engage in meaningful learning. It also creates the conditions within which **positive relationships** can develop and grow within the learning environment. This includes positive relationships between pupils/students themselves and between educators and pupils/students. Indeed, **positive peer affiliation** is also critical for learners to experience a psychologically safe learning environment. The interaction between educators and pupils/students

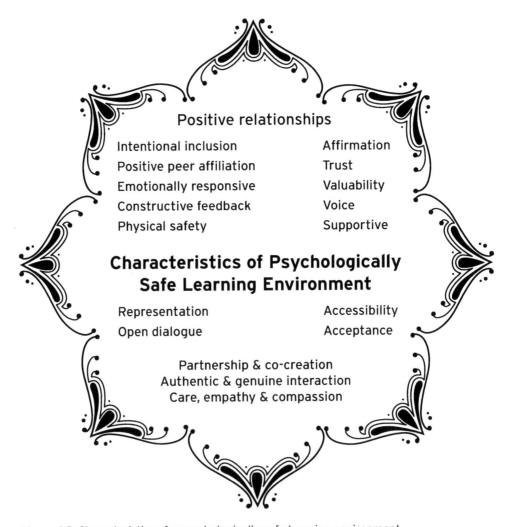

Positive relationships

Intentional inclusion   Affirmation
Positive peer affiliation   Trust
Emotionally responsive   Valuability
Constructive feedback   Voice
Physical safety   Supportive

Characteristics of Psychologically Safe Learning Environment

Representation   Accessibility
Open dialogue   Acceptance

Partnership & co-creation
Authentic & genuine interaction
Care, empathy & compassion

Figure 6.2 Characteristics of a psychologically safe learning environment

also signals how psychologically safe the learning environment is. Interactions characterized by **affirmation, support**, and **constructive feedback** build confidence and self-esteem among learners, encouraging their meaningful engagement in and through the pedagogic encounter. It is also critical that learners feel they have **value** in education – that is, they are valued as their authentic selves by both educators and their peers. **Acceptance** is at the heart of feeling valued. If you feel accepted for who you are, you are affirmed as a valuable member of the learning community. Psychologically safe learning environments also ensure that students can express their **voice(s)** with due regard given to their opinions. **Representation** is also important for helping pupils/students feel that they are a core member of the learning community, while educators work to ensure they have an **intentional approach to inclusion**. This is key to ensuring that all learners feel they belong in the classroom, regardless of their background or needs. **Accessibility** is also important when engaging in intentionally inclusive practices in the classroom. All learners should have equal access to the physical space of the learning environment, the curricular content being taught, the variety of pedagogies employed, and the opportunity to engage with the educator in a positive and affirming manner.

Open dialogue between educator and pupil/student is especially key to nurturing positive and accessible relationships in the classroom, with a multidirectional ebb and flow of communication rather than a didactic approach. A learning environment can only be psychologically safe if an educator can engage positively in an **emotionally responsive way**. This includes answering challenges in a calm and measured way, rather than in a reactive manner, characterized by negative emotions. The more positive the educator's emotional responses are, the greater the psychological safety in the classroom. Of course, it is especially challenging to nurture psychological safety in the absence of **physical safety**. Such environments are unsuitable for learning. It is within psychologically safe learning environments that **authentic and genuine interaction** can be nurtured, creating a space where all members of the learning community (pupils/students and educators) can engage in meaningful **partnership and cocreation** within the classroom. Educaring from the heart calls on educators to place **care, empathy, and compassion** at the heart of their work in creating and nurturing psychologically safe learning environments.

Reflexivity offers educators an opportunity to reflect on pedagogic approaches to identify opportunities to enhance professional practices, the learning environment and relationships with students/pupils. Educators should use the classroom psychological safety audit to reflect on the nature of the learning environment nurtured by your own approaches and practices. It is also an invitation to critically reflect on whether any aspect of your pedagogical approach can be altered or improved to enhance your approach to nurturing a psychologically safe environment with your pupils/students (figure 6.3).

Learning Environment Psychological Safety Audit

| Reflection on practice | Enhancing practice |

Trust

Positive Relationships

Positive Peer Affiliation

Affirmation

Support

Constructive Feedback

Valuability

Acceptance

Voice

Representation

Intentional Inclusion

Accessibility

Open Dialogue

Emotionally Responsive

Physical Safety

Authentic & Genuine Interaction

Partnership & Co-creation

Care, Empathy & Compassion

Figure 6.3 Exercise: Learning environment psychological safety audit

Risk taking is at the heart of teaching and learning. Educators are situated in the juxtaposition between taking risks and facilitating risk taking in the classroom. To engage effectively in teaching and learning it is critical that both educators and students are encouraged to take risks, embracing new curricula through the learning environment. Risk taking requires both learners and educators to push beyond the boundaries of their comfort zone, to embrace challenges and meet each other wholeheartedly through the pedagogic encounter. A failure to embrace risk taking is a failure to nurture and support the flourishing and thriving of our educators and learners in the education system. Educaring from the heart requires educators and students to meet each other in a psychologically safe environment within which vulnerability and risk taking are both valued and encouraged as a key aspect to teaching and learning.

Nurturing in education means caring for the student as they grow and develop as learners and individuals within our society. The work of care and nurture is often hidden in our work as educators across the continuum of education. It can be argued that curricula, pedagogy, and assessment far surpass nurture and care as critical aspects to education across our systems, globally. However, as we witness a decline in the mental wellbeing of our global education communities, it is critical we flip the narrative and focus in education on placing nurturing and caring at the core of our work in both policy and practice. Just like a seed planted in the ground, a student cannot grow in the absence of care and nurture, nor will they ever realise their fullest potential. Indeed, such potential has limitless possibilities when cared for and nurtured in a meaningful and genuine way. For our learners to flourish and thrive, we need to nurture and care for them, meeting and accepting them for who they are when they arrive in our learning environments (figure 6.4).

Educaring from the heart envisages six core aspects to nurturing our students. The first aspect of nurture involves caring for our learners' *hearts*. This means accepting and caring for who they are and how they present to us in the classroom. It means knowing our pupils/students and building an understanding of how they see and interpret the world around them, informed by their own perspectives and understandings. All learners bring with them a broad spectrum of *needs* into the classroom. Nurturing our students means effectively supporting and meeting their individual and collective needs. Sometimes this can be demanding for educators who can be faced with barriers to meeting complex needs in the learning context, including accessing resources or supports for their pupils/students.

Our learners across the continuum of education come into our classrooms with their *aspirations and dreams*. Our role as educators is to nurture our learners in their aspirations and dreams, to encourage them along their life's journey and support them in the development of their self-image and self-esteem. All too often we hear of the power of the 'one good teacher' who has inspired a

Nurturing our Learners

Their heart

Their needs

Their aspirations & dreams

Their life's journey

Their spiritual selves

Their creative being

Figure 6.4 Nurturing our learners in education

child/young person or given them the encouragement they needed to pursue and realise their individual dreams. You can be that one good educator who drops a pebble that makes a positive impact, encouraging their aspirations and dreams with even wider implications for their networks and our society.

Of course, our pupils/students come to our classrooms as they are progressing through their **life journey**. Our role as educators is to meet them where they are in their journey, to support and care for them as best we can, while building their skills and capacities to negotiate the challenges that present to us all in life.

Educaring from the heart also calls on educators to support and nurture the **spiritual self** presented to us by our learners. This includes supporting how they see and understand themselves in the world, how they perceive their greater purpose, and how they manage and look after their own wellbeing in education and beyond.

Finally, educaring from the heart is about nurturing pupil/student **creative being**, from which great transformation can emerge. Creativity empowers both educators and learners to come together in community and to cocreate, explore, and transform the world through their educational interaction. Nurturing educator and pupil/student creativity holds limitless possibilities for transforming our education system and our societies.

The way we, as educators, nurture our learners is by our own experiences and understandings of the world, which we carry in our backpacks into the learning environment. As discussed in chapter 2, being aware of what we carry in our backpacks is critical to helping us understand our own approach to caring for/about and nurturing our students.

Educaring from the heart invites educators to create learning environments wherein students can be cared for and nurtured to flourish, thrive, and realise their fullest potential within education and beyond (Figure 6.5). Such an approach is embedded within care, empathy, and compassion where both learners and educators work in partnership to cocreate positive learning environments characterized by positive relationships.

Nurturing our Learners

How can you nurture the students in your classroom?

Figure 6.5 Exercise: Identifying ways to nurture learners in the learning environment

Educaring from the Heart

Capture your thoughts & feelings here

7 Compassionate Education

Educaring from the heart requires of educators to adopt a compassionate approach in education with care, empathy, and compassion at the core (Figure 7.1).

This triad of care, empathy, and compassion, while similar, are distinct from each other in characteristics and definition, requiring deeper exploration to truly comprehend their importance for educaring from the heart.

Figure 7.1 Educaring from the heart – care, empathy, and compassion

Care is the provision of something necessary to promote the health and welfare of an individual. The caring aspects of education can often lie hidden behind the more overt and visible acts of teaching and learning. Indeed, much of the work of educaring is invisible and undervalued within and across our education systems. Educaring promotes an approach to education where care is realized both within the invisible spaces of our classroom environments, and in/through/with

DOI: 10.4324/9781032718194-9

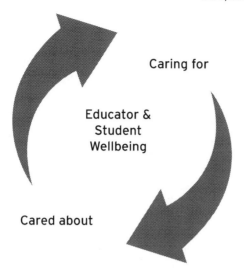

Figure 7.2 Symbiotic relationship between caring for and caring about

the pedagogical approaches we use with our pupils/students. Caring for and being cared about are critical to ensuring we nurture our learners so that they can realise their full potential. The symbiotic relationship between caring for and being cared about characterizes positive and healthy relationships, contributing positively to educator and learner wellbeing alike (Figure 7.2).

This symbiotic relationship between caring for and caring about is mutually beneficial to both student and educator, nourishing the soul and opening hearts to be vulnerable and take risks in the learning environment. Care supports trusting relationships. It is the foundation upon which learners and indeed educators, flourish and thrive in education and beyond. There is nothing more powerful for the individual than being cared for and caring about others. This is especially important within the education system, as educators role model how to receive and give care, which is a key aspect to nurturing compassionate citizenship. Developing competencies and skills in caring will be especially important as pupils/students negotiate a future of uncertainty that will be shaped by climate crises, political unrest, and global patterns of migration. Being cared for and caring about has never been so important in the history of humanity.

Empathy is the ability to understand and share the feelings of another individual. While caring focuses on the provision of something to support someone's wellbeing, empathy deepens our understanding of and relationship to another through meaningful and emotional connection. To empathise, we must be emotionally literate to both express our feelings and understand and share the feelings of others. In validating the feelings of others, including our pupils/students, we are validating their experiences and how they understand themselves, as they navigate the complexity of the world around them. The ability to empathise and express oneself, drawing on emotional literacy, is especially important in our increasingly complex worlds where societal challenges intersect with our daily lives. Our classrooms are microcosms that bear witness to this need, whether it is expressed as increasing anxiety about climate change or a deep sadness or anger in response to life circumstances. Indeed, at times and for some educators, the classroom can be a volatile environment where emotions are bubbling beneath the surface and sometimes breaking through in the classroom space. It is in these instances that educators draw on the relationships they have built with their pupils/students to respond in an empathetic way. This can be especially challenging if such emotional expressions manifest as anger or physical expression. Empathy is at the core of educaring from the heart because individuals feel truly understood and seen within the education system when their feelings are recognized and validated. This is especially important in circumstances where a student may be disengaged because they feel isolated or marginalized within the education system. Adopting an empathetic approach can open hearts and possibilities for reengagement by rebuilding trust of the education system. We especially see the power of an empathetic approach in more alternative and/or informal approaches to supporting students who have been failed by the more formal education system through attrition or exclusion. Investing time in empathy when working with pupils/students not only helps to support them and their learning in the system, it also models how to adopt an empathetic approach in life, which can only contribute positively to our wider societies and world.

Compassion is our emotional response to empathy. It includes taking action in response to empathizing with an individual's situation. Fundamentally, compassion begins with a conversation to identify what the individual needs in response to the challenges they face. Such compassionate dialogue occurs in and through the daily interactions between educator and pupil/student. It underpins the relational dynamics enhancing the work of the educator and, hence, the learning experiences in the classroom. Educators are especially skilled at identifying pupils/students who may be in emotional distress/turmoil. Compassionate responses, given in a time sensitive manner, are critical to supporting learners as they navigate their emotional distress/turmoil, and to avoid the unintentional or unnecessary conflict that often arises in emotionally tense or volatile situations (Figure 7.3).

It is critical that educators are equipped with the skills to be able to take a compassionate approach, including the ability to (a) **identify** when a student may be in distress, (b) **respond** to such distress/turmoil in a time-sensitive manner, (c) use **compassionate dialogue** as a means to identify challenges and needs, (d) **apply** compassionate responses to support the students, and (e) provide and **sustain** ongoing supports for students who find themselves in such challenging circumstances.

Educaring from the Heart-Compassionate Approach

Identify

Respond

Dialogue

Apply

Sustain

Figure 7.3 Educaring from the heart - compassionate approach

This next exercise invites you to pause and consider how you adopt a compassionate approach in your practice as an educator. Reflect on your own experiences as an educator, drawing on examples of situations or circumstances where a compassionate response was required. How did you respond? Was there anything different you would do to adopt a more compassionate approach with your pupil/student if you could respond again to that situation or circumstance? What compassionate approaches do you find most useful in your own practice? Have there been situations/circumstances where your compassionate approach did not work? Why was this? Is there something you could have done to overcome challenges to responding in a compassionate way? Educaring from the heart is an invitation to consider how best to embed compassionate approaches in your teaching as an educator when working with children/young people/adults across the continuum of education (Figure 7.4).

The intersection of care, empathy, and compassion underpins educaring from the heart (Figure 7.5).

While care is the provision of something an individual needs, empathy is the ability to understand and share the feelings of an individual. Compassion is the

Reflecting on your Compassionate Approach as Educator

Working Well

Barriers/
Challenges

Approaches to
Try

Figure 7.4 Exercise: Reflecting on your compassionate approach as educator

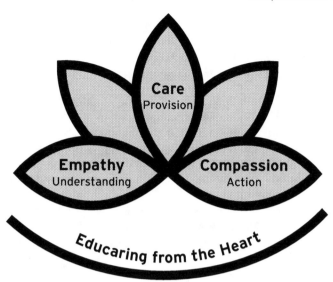

Figure 7.5 The intersection of care, empathy, and compassion

dynamic action taken in response to an individual's circumstance or situation. Educaring from the heart adopts a compassionate approach to supporting pupils/ students as they navigate the complexities of challenges in their lives.

Why does compassionate education matter? In human history, the world has never been so complex and interdependent. The information age has brought positives (such as immediate access to information and means of communication, transformative digital technologies) and negatives (such as the intrusion, consumption of time, lack of regulation and the spread of misinformation) that directly impact how we experience our lives. Indeed, it is no coincidence that, with the emergence of the information age, we have witnessed an increase in levels of anxiety among children, young people, and within our wider societies. The intensification of time has been particularly notable, evident in the increasing demands made of our time in both our educational and personal lives. This is also true for the learners in our classrooms.

Most notable of all has been the erosion and devaluing of the importance of doing nothing with our time. Taking time to be in silence and solitude is an important aspect of restoring our wellbeing and helping us to reengage with the world in a meaningful way. It also helps us to avoid the very real risk of burnout in our lives. However, the value of doing nothing has somehow been eroded for us as educators, but it has most especially been eroded for the children/young people/individuals we teach in our learning environments. A key factor in accounting for the effective use of our time is the increasing dependence on social media to validate our use of time through approval or likes on social media. Indeed, such social media validation has become an extremely damaging way for individuals (especially children and young people) to measure their worth or value. The problem is that the measure of value is continuously shifting and individuals are measured according to unrealistic expectations that arise from what is defined and valued as a productive citizen in our complex worlds. This includes value judgements about how we live, the values we hold, the aesthetics of how we look, the social networks and relationships we access. Our pupils/students are navigating the complexities of these social worlds, carrying them with them as they journey through the education system. The exterior world has never been so compressed and internalized as it currently is.

Our learning environments are microcosms of the broader social worlds within which they are located. They reflect the context in which our learners live, and which they bring to their interactions with pedagogy, curriculum, and the learning environment. For some learners, this means bringing the complexities of their lives. As educators practicing compassionate education, it is vital we have an awareness of such complexities, which often manifest their manner of engaging in learning and interacting with others. Educaring from the heart calls on educators to accept wholeheartedly the student in front of them and support them with compassion when the complexities of their life challenges manifest in the classroom. When such issues cannot be supported or resolved in the classroom, it is imperative that we enter into compassionate dialogue to identify the needs and corresponding resources our pupils/students need to support them in reaching their fullest potential in and across our education system.

Over the past couple of decades, we have witnessed significant progress in the identification of needs among our learners in our classrooms. We now have more sophisticated approaches to identifying additional learner needs at earlier stages in the education system. While significant gaps in this identification system and process still exist, the opportunity for early intervention means that children and young people will do significantly better on their educational trajectories. Educaring from the heart means that each child is valued equally within the education system, regardless of any additional need they have. Indeed, failure to support the learner in an equitable way is a failure of the system, and not the child/young person who is deemed to be failing within the system. This is a fundamental principle underpinning the educaring from the heart approach, a principle that is often espoused in the institutional mottos and/or values of educational institutions across our systems. While the messaging around educational inclusion is important for valuing all learners equally, what is more important is how these values are realized in our pedagogical practices in our classrooms. Educaring from the heart calls on educators to ensure that all learners are included, represented, and recognized in the work we do with them in our interactions, pedagogy, curriculum, and the assessment approaches we use. Failure to do this, is a failure of the system to meet and respond to the needs of all students in the classroom.

However, the greatest threat to this idealized description of inclusive practice in our educational institutions is lack of time and resources. Often we do not have control over access to time and resources and we are dependent on policies and procedures to provide us with what we need to support our learners' needs in our learning environments. This includes continuous professional development opportunities, practical resources, additional personnel/educational practitioners, access to testing, and external professional bodies (such as educational psychologists, occupational therapists, speech and language therapists etc.) to ensure we meet our learners' needs in a meaningful and effective manner. The intensification of demands on educators' time, most especially to support learner needs either reactively (in moments of challenge) or proactively (planning for supports), means that there is very little (if any) time for effective planning for and reflection on the high demands made of educators. The erosion of time in education is one of the greatest threats to our education system in this era. It undermines the importance of trusting educators to use their time effectively to deliver the curriculum while supporting learners in the classroom. Indeed, the bureaucratization of education in the form of paperwork and accountability, especially for educational leaders, is increasingly interfering with the nature of educator-learner interaction within our systems. While there is a balance to be struck between purposeful planning for effective teaching and learning and meeting the needs of learners, increasing paperwork can hinder the applied work of educators in the classroom, directing time away from learners and onto paperwork for accountability. This issue is particularly pertinent to school leaders, who are charged with leading teaching and learning in a school, yet often find themselves grappling with a quagmire of administrative paperwork that directs them away from the very task for which they are appointed.

There has never been a more important time in education to slow down in order to make more meaningful progress across our system, for ourselves as educators and leaders and our pupils/students. Educaring from the heart requires that educators are entrusted with both agency and time to engage in compassionate education, placing the learner and their needs at the heart of the education system, while at the same time accepting and valuing them for who they are in our classrooms. As a final step in this chapter, I invite you to do a care audit of your classroom. As a prompt, the invitation is to reflect on practices you currently employ to care for the students in your classroom and to identify some approaches you will adopt to embed care, empathy, and compassion into your work with your learners (Figure 7.6).

Compassionate education is embedded within the power of the relationships, a core aspect to educaring from the heart that we will now explore in the next chapter.

Educaring from the Heart Care Audit

Approaches to care
working well

Approaches to care
to try

Figure 7.6 Exercise: Educaring from the heart care audit

Educaring from the Heart

Capture your thoughts & feelings here

8 The Power of Relational Pedagogy

Education is deeply embedded within the power of the relational dynamics in the learning environment. Relationships form the cornerstone of the pedagogic encounter between educator and student. The quality of that relationship directly shapes the interactions and engagement levels of the learning environment. Educaring from the heart can only truly be realized through the power of positive relationships in the learning environment, which ensure our children and young people flourish and thrive. Indeed, high quality positive relationships are the lynch-pin upon which our education systems and wider societies flourish and thrive. The EDUCARE principles of the educaring from the heart approach to relationships are presented in Figure 8.1 and include: (a) engagement and dialogue, (b) delight and curiosity, (c) understanding and empathy, (d) connection and compassion, (e) authenticity and acceptance, (f) respect and trust, and (e) equity and inclusion.

Educaring from the heart begins with **engagement and dialogue**. Meaningful engagement with those around us is fundamental to building relationships. This calls us to be vulnerable in creating the optimal conditions to engage with our pupils/students and our wider educational communities. Dialogue is critical to enabling meaningful engagement. It ensures that all parties have an opportunity to share their views and be understood. As such, it is important that dialogue is multi-directional, ebbing and flowing between individuals, building on views and ideas, and - critically - incorporating such views into decisions and/or actions that impact all parties involved. While evidence would indicate that dialogue happens more now within the structures of education (from student councils to policy making consultative forums) than in the past, there is still much work to be done to incorporate dialogue into education. Providing time and space for educators to dialogue with policy makers is especially important for ensuring we have a responsive, relevant, and dynamic education system. There is still much progress to be made to provide both educators and pupils/students with equal opportunity for dialogue in our education system.

DOI: 10.4324/9781032718194-10

Educaring from the Heart
The Power of the Relational

Engagement & Dialogue

Delight & Curiosity

Understanding & Empathy

Connection & Compassion

Authenticity & Acceptance

Respect & Trust

Equity & Inclusion

Figure 8.1 EDUCARE relational principles

Educaring from the heart calls on educators to take ***delight and curiosity*** when working with pupils/students. Educators hold a privileged position in our societies, and within the lives of our children and young people. We are entrusted not only to educate our pupils/students, but also to care for them. Taking delight in our pupils/students, being curious about who they are now, as well as who they grow and develop to be is an important aspect of educaring from the heart. Maintaining that delight and curiosity as we progress through our careers can be challenging at times, especially at pinch points when we feel overloaded or overwhelmed. In those moments, it is important to return to the reason why your journey has brought you to education and explore how you can reconnect with your purpose as an educator. As educators, taking delight in our pupils/students and being curious about them is integral to nurturing an environment within which they can flourish and thrive.

Understanding and empathy underpins the development and nurturing of relationships in education. When pupils/students feel understood they are more likely to engage in education. Empathy facilitates understanding and allows for deeper and more meaningful relationships in the learning environment. Engaging with students and taking a delightful and curious approach to getting to know who they are as individuals builds empathy and understanding, contributing to more positive relationships and, hence, more meaningful and effective learning experiences.

While engagement and dialogue create the relational conditions within which we can take delight and curiosity in/with our students, understanding and empathy bring us to a deeper, more meaningful place of **connection** with and **compassion** for our students. Connecting at a relational level in education is particularly important for nurturing the wellbeing of our students by supporting their psychosocial and emotional development through positive attachment to and relationships with us as educators. It is through meaningful connection that educators can take a compassionate approach to their pupils/students, by identifying and supporting their needs in a proactive and positive way.

Authenticity and acceptance is an important aspect of building relationships when educaring from the heart. Being accepted for who you are is a powerful and empowering experience for any individual, but most especially for the pupils/students. We cannot overestimate the impact of being seen and accepted for who we are, and the powerful and lifelong impact it can have on an individual in education. 'One good adult' in our lives can make a powerful impact on us as humans. Equally, the power of 'one good teacher' to make a difference in an individual's life is profound, and often, this difference is very much connected to the feeling of being seen and accepted for who you are. Being authentic with pupils/students nurtures genuine, caring, and compassionate relationships in the learning environment and beyond. Indeed, it is the most powerful way of communicating meaningful compassion for and acceptance of the children and young people with whom we work as educators.

Respect and trust must be nurtured within a positive learning environment in order to create the optimal conditions for realizing our EDUCARE principles. Optimal learning occurs in learning environments with psychological safety, which is manifested through feelings of trust between the educator and the learner. Engaging in teaching and learning is a vulnerable act, where both educator and learner take risks to open themselves and their hearts to new information and experiences that must be negotiated through the power of relational pedagogy. Trust is at the heart of this interaction, and deep and meaningful learning will only occur when pupils/students feel they can trust the learning environment – and this can only happen when they trust the educator. Trust is nurtured through respect. When learners feel respected, they are more likely to approach the learning encounter in a more open and authentic manner. Respect also breeds respect. Demonstrating respect for our learners contributes to a more respectful and positive relationship with them. It also ensures they feel affirmed in who they are as individuals, and contributes positively to their holistic development, which is a key aspect of educaring from the heart.

The final EDUCARE principle underpins the work we strive to do as educators to promote and realize a more equitable and inclusive society for all individuals, regardless of race, ethnicity, gender, dis/ability, socioeconomic status, sexual identity, and so on. This work begins in and through the education system. Educaring from the heart places particular emphasis on the importance of adopting policies and practices that realise **equity and inclusion** in our learning environments and across our education system. Educators work hard to make a positive difference in the lives of those with whom they work, and equity and inclusion are never far from how they approach that work in planning and practice. Educaring from the heart calls on educators to continue to enhance the work they do in education to support and include all learners in the classroom. Furthermore, it requires us to identify and call out any shortcomings when our system fails our pupils/students in any way. The most damaging outcome affecting learners is that they feel they have failed. This is especially damaging for those learners coming from the most marginalized groups within our societies who must, at times, battle against complex and multilayered structural inequalities to succeed in education. As educators, it is our ethical and moral responsibility to highlight and call out systemic failures and contribute to identifying ways to break down the barriers that prevent or challenge equitable access to education for all.

The EDUCARE principles provide a framework against which any educator, working across the continuum of education, can reflect and consider their own approach to building the relational aspects of their practice when educaring from the heart. It is an invitation also to reflect on the EDUCARE relational principles that most strongly speak to your own heart and how you nurture everyone in your own classroom/learning environment. Perhaps there are principles you would like to explore in more depth with your own pupils/students to enhance and deepen your own relational practice in the classroom? The following template provides an opportunity to reflect on your own approach to nurturing the relational in the learning environment drawing on the EDUCARE principles (Figure 8.2).

We cannot underestimate the power of relational pedagogy to provide limitless transformational possibilities to our children and young people in the classroom. When educaring from the heart, we invest time into deeply reflecting upon and considering our approach to building the relational aspects of our work as educators. The outcome of investing in nurturing positive relationships is beneficial for all members of the learning community, including pupils/students and educators. Nurturing positive relationships enhances engagement in learning and contributes to enhanced wellbeing for all members within the learning environment. Relational pedagogy is a cornerstone upon which the work of teaching, learning and assessment can be built, scaffolding more positive engagement and affiliation with school. It also contributes to building a greater sense of belonging within the education system.

**EDUCARE Principles
My personal reflection**

Engagement & Dialogue

Delight & Curiosity

Understanding & Empathy

Connection & Compassion

Authenticity & Acceptance

Respect & Trust

Equity & Inclusion

Figure 8.2 Exercise: EDUCARE principles personal reflection

Being affirmed and accepted for who you are is critical to communicating a sense of belonging to students as they navigate their way through our education systems. Indeed, the stronger that sense of belonging within the education system, the more positive the academic and psychosocial outcomes for learners.

While educaring from the heart seeks to educate with heart, it also seeks to educate the heart of learners in the classroom as they engage as active citizens in the world around them. Navigating and negotiating the relational aspects of our lives will be especially important in an increasingly complex and globalized world. Relationships are the foundation upon which creative solutions to challenges are identified and applied. It is critical to the flourishing and thriving of humanity and, as such, it is imperative that our pupils/students experience a positive approach to relationships in order to build and nurture positive relationships within and across our societies. How better to learn about and experience relationships than within the safety of positive learning environments?

Educaring from the Heart

Capture your thoughts & feelings here

9 Empowering Voices

Educaring from the heart is an invitation to a democratic approach to education where the voices of learners are listened to, heard, and acted upon. Voice is central to taking a democratic approach to education. I use the plural *voices* in this chapter to recognise the multiplicity and heterogeneity of voices among our children and young people, who are more often than not perceived as a homogenous group. Whether working with children, young people, or adult learners, the embedding of voices within our practices as educators can contribute to increased engagement in the learning environment, enhanced educator and learner wellbeing, and greater autonomy and ownership in the learning process. Voices also contribute to holistic development of the child and young person as active citizens of the world. Active citizenship is increasingly more important as we continue to be challenged by the many complexities of living in our contemporary worlds. Nurturing the agency of children and youth is critical to empowering them to make a positive contribution to changemaking in the world around them. Empowering their voices is the mechanism through which children and young people can contribute to changemaking in their schools, communities, and beyond.

Voice is an important aspect of ensuring a democratic approach to education. Article 12 of the UN Convention on the Rights of the Child (UNCRC) enshrines the importance of children's views in matters affecting them, stating:

> States Parties shall assure to the child who is capable of forming his or her own views the right to express those views freely in all matters affecting the child, the views of the child being given due weight in accordance with the age and maturity of the child.

While the UNCRC enshrines the right for children to share their voices in institutions, such as education, what is lacking is the *how*: how do we ensure children and young people can share their voices in education, and - perhaps more critically - how do we ensure we respond to and, more importantly, act upon their voices in a meaningful

DOI: 10.4324/9781032718194-11

way? Lundy's model for participation provides a practical framework that can be used across institutions to support and meaningfully engage with children's voices and is increasingly in evidence across education systems internationally. The four key components of Lundy's model espouse the importance of space (providing a safe and inclusive space for children to share their views), voice (supporting children to express their views), audience (providing opportunity for children to share their views with decision makers), and influence (taking children's views seriously and acting upon them as appropriate) in meaningfully realising children's participation in decision-making about issues directly impacting their lives (Lundy, 2007). Lundy's model of participation provides a solid framework for empowering children's voices in education.

While much progress has been made in incorporating children and young people's voices into education, including the increasing prevalence of pupil/student councils across all levels of schooling, there yet remains many opportunities and possibilities for empowering voices across the continuum of education. The EDUCARE principles provide an educationally focussed framework for empowering voices in and across education (Figure 9.1).

EDUCARE Principles for Empowering Voice(s)

Valued

Openhearted

Inclusive

Collaborative

Enacted

Supported

Figure 9.1 EDUCARE principles for empowering voices

When educaring from the heart, it is important that children and young people's voices are **valued** and respected for what they have to say and how and when they say it. It is especially important we create rituals in education to ensure that learners' voices are encouraged, cultivated, cared for, and acted upon. Such rituals can be formal in nature, including the use of class, student, or institutional councils that encourage learners to participate in decision-making processes at the micro- and macrolevel of the educational context. However, it is important not to make the mistake of negating the power of more informal approaches to empowering voices in our learning environments. This includes providing the conditions and opportunities for learners to participate in shaping what it is they learn (curriculum), how they learn (through pedagogical practices), and the approaches to assessment adopted as part of the educational encounter in the classroom. Embedding practices that empower voices in/through/with pedagogical approaches in the classroom offers transformative possibilities for both learners and educators, while also contributing to the holistic development of the child/young person as an active citizen with agency and power to create change(s) in the education system and our broader society.

Adopting an **openhearted** approach to empowering voices in education is critical to nurturing an open and safe environment within which children and young people feel they can share their opinions and ideas without fear of any repercussions or belittlement. Being open to different views and perspectives can be challenging, especially as educators, where teaching is deeply entwined with our personal lives – our own identities and how we understand who we are as educators. Receiving feedback on how we do our work and how we interact with the pupils/students in front of us can cut deep into the core of our being, particularly if such feedback challenges us and our own perception of ourselves as educators. However, being open to engaging in an openhearted way can be rewarding for both educator and pupil/student, creating a more collaborative dialogue to enhance teaching and learning.

Voices should always be **inclusive**. This is especially true in an increasingly globalised world characterised by more diverse and multicultural populations, which are reflected in classrooms across our education institutions and systems. As such, ensuring an inclusive approach to empowering voices in education is so important to educaring from the heart. As educators, it is critical to reflect on the voices we listen to, hear and act upon in education and whether they are representative of the spectrum of identities across our pupil/student population including, but not limited to, gender, ethnicity, dis/ability, social class etc. Voices represent belonging. To be listened to and heard in education is to affirm belonging within the system. Adopting an inclusive approach to empowering voices ensures that all children and young people are represented and affirmed in their belonging within the system and within our societies more broadly. Voice also attributes power. Adopting an inclusive approach to voices in education is to redistribute power and ensure a more equitable learning environment for all. The ripple impact of this across our societies cannot be underestimated.

Voices within the educaring framework should be **collaborative**, constantly in flux, flowing, and multidirectional, with all members of the learning community provided with equal opportunities to engage and participate in reflection and ideation. Collaboration demands working as a collective within the learning community, working in partnership to build ideas, identify opportunities, and engage critically in a process of reflexivity on practices and approaches within the classroom. Consensus building is a critical aspect to collaborative voice, especially when making a decision or prioritising the most pertinent issue for the learning community at any particular time. Education systems, and hence the people working within them, have an ethical and moral responsibility to ensure we provide an equitable platform for voices. Creating safe spaces for the inclusion of all voices in a collaborative process within a learning community is critical to providing and supporting a platform for all voices in education more broadly.

Voices are only truly empowered when they are **enacted**. Educaring from the heart calls on educators and educational institutions to ensure they not only listen to and hear pupil/student voices, but also enact the suggestions and ideas they share as appropriate. One of the limitations to pupil/student voice in education is tokenism. This arises when pupil/student voices are listened to and heard but are not taken seriously enough to be enacted through meaningful actions, such as making changes or addressing issues of concern expressed by children and young people. It is critical to move away from more tokenistic approaches to voices in order to incorporate pupil/student voices in education in a more meaningful and proactive way.

The final principle for empowering voice through educaring is to ensure that students are **supported** in and through the process. The educator plays a key role in supporting pupils/students in sharing and enacting their voices in education. This requires of the educator to provide the opportunities for supporting pupil/student voices in and through the pedagogic encounter. Care, empathy, and compassion, at the core of the educaring from the heart ethic, is fundamental to ensuring that students feel supported in sharing their voices in education. Key to this is identifying the opportunities for enabling voices in education - conceptualised as the Five Ps for voice in education within the educaring from the heart approach (Figure 9.2).

Finding the opportunity for embedding voices into education can be challenging when working within the busyness of the classroom environment. Educaring from

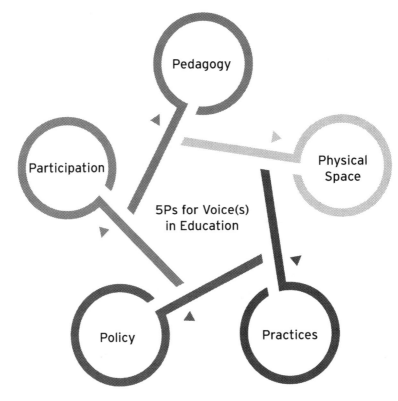

Figure 9.2 Five Ps for voices in education

the heart proffers the Five Ps for embedding opportunities for voices in education, including: (1) pedagogy, (2) physical space, (3) practices in educational institutions, (4) policy, and (5) participation.

The increasing emphasis on the importance of children's/young people's voices in education is to be welcomed. However, it is important to consider that embedding voices in education need not be a separate undertaking to the work in/through/with **pedagogy**. Indeed, pedagogy, the everyday formal and informal interactions between educator and pupil/student in the classroom, provides fertile ground within which voices can be grown and nurtured in everyday classroom interactions. Pedagogy is defined by educational interactions, methodologies, and approaches, and is mediated through the relational aspects of our work as educators. Embedding voices into these momentary and every day formal and informal interactions serves to empower voices, particularly for pupils/students. Table 9.1 provides an overview of the ways student voices can be embedded into our pedagogical practices as educators.

Table 9.1 Empowering voices in/through/with pedagogy

Empowering Voices in/through/with Pedagogy Students/pupils are afforded choice on:		
Topics/curriculum to be explored	Methodologies to be used	Assessment procedures
Setting up the learning environment	Content to be included	The learning journey as it evolves
The resources to be used	Discussion topics and approaches	Learning outcomes
The terms for engaging and interacting with each other	The timing of learning	The learning process
The product of learning	The composition of the learning community	Feedback and grading
Review and reflection on the learning process and their experience of voices	How to share best practice as they have experienced it	Sharing/Evaluating their experience with the educator and engagement with pedagogy

Embedding voices in/though/with pedagogy proffers a democratic approach to education where pupils/students are empowered in and through the everyday formal and informal interactions in the classroom. Such an approach requires educators to be open and flexible, willing to take risks in transferring the balance of pedagogic power from teacher to pupil/student, based on age appropriateness and ability to make informed decisions.

Physical space can impact how we empower student/pupil voices in education. Power is transmitted through physical spaces, either hindering or enabling the realisation of pupil/student voices in and across our educational institutions. There are two aspects to empowering voices through physical space in an educational setting: (a) using space and (b) creating space. Using the physical spaces of education are critical to empowering voices. This can be especially challenging when the physical space available is restrictive or hinders the ability of educators to afford opportunities to facilitate voices. For example, a room that holds a large number of pupils/students (such as a large classroom or lecture theatre) can be an intimidating place for both educators and pupils/students to facilitate/express voices. Equally, a classroom where there is little physical space to move around and engage in a free and open manner can be counterproductive to rebalancing the pedagogic power and facilitating voices in the learning environment. The furniture and resources available to pupils/students and educators can also serve to constrict or enable the possibilities for voices. Educaring from the heart calls on educators to use physical space to facilitate voices, even in situations where it can be especially challenging.

The second aspect of voices relates to the creation of physical space to empower pupils/students within and across our education systems. Creating space for voices is essential in the everyday practices of the educational setting. Creating a physical space dedicated to empowering voices is especially important in educaring from the heart. It recognises the importance of enshrining Article 12 of the UN Convention on the Rights of the Child (UNCRC) in the physical spaces of our education system, providing children and young people with formal opportunities to share their opinions in a safe and authentic way. The physical spaces in and between our educational institutions play a critical role in empowering pupil/student voices. The way in which physical space is used and created serves an important role to supporting our children and young people to flourish and thrive as global citizens, cared about and for in our education system and beyond. Figure 9.3 provides an invitation to conduct an audit of space for empowering voices in your own educational context.

Practices in education make a significant contribution to the purpose, nature, and empowering of pupil/student voices across educational institutions. The way we practice pupil/student voices in education significantly contributes to the way our children and young people understand their identities and agency as citizens within our societies. It is essential to equip our children and young people with the skills, knowledge, and – most crucial of all – confidence to use their voices as an expression of their agency within our education systems and across our societies more broadly.

Indeed, educational practices are shaped and informed by **policy**, a particularly important aspect to realising and empowering voices in/through/with education. Policy defines expectations for educational practices and the nature of the work we undertake as educators in our institutions. Policy makers at the macro- (international and national) and microlevels (educational institutions including early years' settings, schools, tertiary education) are charged with responsibility to shape what happens in the everyday lives of our children and young people, and as such are powerful actors in determining curricular content delivered, pedagogical practices employed, and the nature of interactions within and across these learning environments. As such, policy can work to empower or, unintentionally, disempower voices within education. While much work has been undertaken to recognise the importance of pupil/student voices in educational policy, there is a gap in measuring the level to which learner voices have been enacted and realised in/through/with educational policies and practices in our educational institutions. While policy can act to guide the educator in effectively empowering voices in their educational setting, it can also serve as an enabler by promoting and enshrining the importance of voices in education. Policy universalises the importance of voices across educational institutions and settings, and as such there is much work to be done to strengthen such policies globally to ensure we realise the potential for children and young people's voices within education. Failure to continue to build on policy to support and realise pupil/student voices in education is a failure to support the full and holistic development of our children and young people as agentic citizens within our societies.

Learning Environment for Voice(s) Audit

Reflection on practice	Enhancing practice

Free movement for all

Distribution of power

All voices heard

Quiet space to listen

Neutral space

Furniture

Accessibility

Facilitating inclusion

Expression of voice(s)

Multiple approaches

Comfort

Welcoming

Learner-centric

Safe

Figure 9.3 Exercise: An audit of the learning environment for empowering voices

Embedding voice(s) & participation in your learning environment

Reflection on practice	Enhancing practice

How do you demonstrate you value young people in your learning environment?

How do you engage with young people in authentic ways?

How do you facilitate open and two-way communication in your learning environment?

How do you ensure psychological safety for facilitating voice(s) and participation in your practice and approach?

How do you demonstrate care/empathy/compassion for your students?

Figure 9.4 Exercise: Embedding voices & participation in your learning environment

The practices and policies we employ in our education systems play a critical role in shaping agentic global citizens who are empowered to make changes and address challenges in our increasingly complex and interdependent world. Much of this foundational work begins the moment a child enters into and transitions through our education systems. Educaring from the heart requires that our educational institutions ensure that policies and practice serve to empower the voices of those at the heart of our education systems – our children and young people. Meaningful empowerment of learner voices cannot be realised in the absence of policy supporting practices across our institutions.

Finally, empowering voices in and of itself is not enough. It is vital to respond to and act upon voices in a meaningful and authentic way. As such, it is important that we, as educators, enact voices through meaningful and productive **participation**. Such participation is critical to nurture active citizenship among our children and young people as influential agents for change in the world around them. Participation is also critical in communicating the importance and value of children/young people's contribution to our societies in the present, rather than solely for the future. In order to nurture participation, we need to ensure the conditions for such engagement are optimal. This includes valuing children and young people, engaging in authentic and genuine ways, using open and two-way communication, ensuring psychological safety, caring for and about them, and engaging in an empathetic and compassionate way. These are fundamental principles for nurturing voices and participation when educaring from the heart.

The following exercise is an invitation to reflect on your own role as an educator in facilitating voices and participation in your learning environment. Use the prompts provided in Figure 9.4 to guide you in reflecting on current practice and possible opportunities to enhance voices and participation in your own learning environment.

This chapter has explored the importance of empowering voices in education when educaring from the heart underpinned by the principles of VOICE; value, openheartedness, inclusivity, collaboration, enaction and support. The possibilities for the empowerment of children/young people's voices through the educaring approach proffer opportunities to truly support and realise authentic voices in/through/with pedagogy, physical space, practices, policy, and participation in education. The next section of this book will explore the progression in the educare approach, moving from the "I" (separate from the other) to the "Us" (existing side by side) and finally to the "We" (coming together in partnership as cocreators within the learning environment). This will now be explored in more depth in the next section.

References

Lundy, L. (2007). '"Voice" is not enough: Conceptualising Article 12 of the United Nations Convention on the rights of the child.' *British Educational Research Journal*, 33(6), 927–942.

Educaring from the Heart

Capture your thoughts & feelings here

Part 3: The "We" as Cocreators for Wellbeing

10 Cocreating Heart-full Education

Coming together in partnership to cocreate heart-full education in our learning environments epitomizes a true realization of educaring from the heart. Challenging and overcoming hegemonic and longstanding pedagogic practices that place the educator in a position of power regarding content presented, approach taken, and learning outcomes valued devolves the fulcrum of power from the all-knowing educator to empower a coming together of community of practice in unity. Educaring from the heart demands educators consciously work to redistribute this hegemonic power within a shared learning community. It is in the coming together as "we" that truly heart-full education can be realized.

Cocreating in education can be considered a creative process, empowering both educator and learner while also nurturing wellbeing in the learning environment. Taking this more democratic approach to pedagogy places child/learner rights at the core of the learning process, contributing to increased pupil/student motivation and engagement, deeper learning opportunities and experiences, and enhanced engagement with creativity, innovation, and critical thinking, while also nurturing more democratic autonomous learning that contributes to increased confidence and self-esteem. Quite simply, cocreative classrooms place the child/young person at the heart of learning. The educator facilitates and guides the learner through this process of cocreation, scaffolding the framework for learning, while at the same time empowering learners to direct the content and outcome. Table 10.1 demonstrates the characteristics of a cocreative learning environment.

Sharing and rebalancing/redistribution of power is at the core of cocreating heart-full education. It takes courage and vulnerability to create environments that shift the distribution of power from the educator to the learner, which requires that the education institutional culture is supportive and proactive of such an approach. This is challenging for education, which traditionally has been perceived as a conservative profession. The traditional chalk-and-talk or sage-on-the-stage

DOI: 10.4324/9781032718194-13

Table 10.1 Characteristics of a cocreative learning environment

Characteristics of a cocreative learning environment	
Sharing and rebalance/distribution of power	Mutual Respect
Free expression and two-way dialogue	Movement and Flow
Psychological safety	Care, empathy, and compassion
Dynamic and responsive	Engagement and enthusiasm
Multidirectional teaching and learning	All community contributions equally valued
Risk and vulnerability	Creativity and innovation
Critical-thinking skills	Learner-centric pedagogy

approach is still dominant and influential in the pedagogical practices of our educational institutions. As such, both educators and educational institutions can fear this approach to redistribute the power of teaching and learning, which redefines how we understand education in our systems. Adopting a learner-centric approach to teaching and learning, whereby the voice of the child/young person is listened to and acted upon can be perceived as threatening to the status of order and control within these complex environments. Indeed, order and control are traditionally perceived as essential components of effective teaching and learning. However, shifting the balance of power from teacher to learner results in more engaged, deeper, and real-life learning, promoting the development of skills such as critical thinking, problem solving, collaborative learning, and reflection. Empathy is at the core of such devolvement of power from educator to child/young person, because it is necessary to identify where the learner is and what the learning journey is they wish to lead in the classroom. Educaring from the heart encourages educators across the continuum of education to rebalance the distribution of power in the learning environment to truly place the learners and their needs at the heart of the learning process.

Educaring from the heart promotes the importance of **mutual respect** when cocreating learning in the classroom. The adage of giving respect to earn respect is especially pertinent in this instance. While it is important that there is a sense of respect from children/young people when working in cocreative ways, this is often nurtured by a respectful approach adopted by educator. It takes the educator to model and authentically engage in a respectful way in order for children/young people also to strive for respect in their engagements in the classroom. Creating and nurturing learning environments where such mutual respect can thrive is critical when educaring from the heart.

Mutual respect creates a space for **free expression and mutual dialogue**, a key aspect to cocreating learning in the classroom. Both educator and learner are interacting within the deeply complex social worlds that exist between and around them. As such, navigating these environments can be challenging because they are embedded within a complex matrix of power dynamics and relational histories. When educaring from the heart, it is important for educators to nurture a learning environment that allows, facilitates, and supports free expression from children/young people, as well as ensuring that dialogue occurs in a multidirectional manner as illustrated in Figure 10.1. Cocreation of learning flourishes when the parameters framing social interaction within the learning environment are malleable and responsive to all participants, including both learners and educators alike.

Cocreation within a learning environment thrives when there is free **movement and flow** within and between the physical, relational, and educational spaces of the classroom. This aspect of cocreation is crucial to ensuring that both educator and learner can reach their full potential as creative agents co-leading the learning in the classroom. Navigating the physical environment is especially key to creating the conditions within which cocreation can be facilitated. Cocreation ideally occurs within a physical environment that can respond to the needs of learner and educator as the learning progresses. This includes the ability to alter the physical environment by moving furniture, or the learners themselves, to create a space where free and meaningful engagement and interaction can occur. Encouraging the development of relationships through cocreation is especially important. This includes the relationship with self, and with others in the learning environment. Cocreating heart-full education nurtures empathy, and compassion, allowing

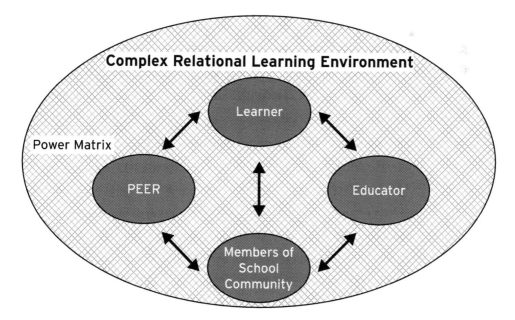

Figure 10.1 Cocreating the learning environment when educaring from the heart

for an enhancement of relationships between educators, learners, and all those participating at any given time. Moving and flowing between these complex relational dynamics also afford the opportunity to ensure an inclusive approach to learning by nurturing greater empathy and understanding between all members of the learning community. Shared experiences and understanding can result in the enhancement and strengthening of relationships between all those navigating the complexity of social dynamics. Cocreative classrooms work to neutralize the value of educational spaces in the learning environment. If pupils/students can freely move between and within the educational spaces associated with learning, the hierarchical, academic-ability structures that operate within the learning environment can be challenged, and at best neutralized. Cocreative learning arises in/ through/with relationships in the classroom. As learners work together, supported by the educator, the focus shifts from a deficit model of learning to a more positive strengths-based approach where the responsibility for learning is shared in and between learners as they navigate the educational tasks set for them. Cocreating a heart-full education means that all learners are valued as equal contributors to the learning process. As such, they move and flow between these educational spaces without any academic barrier preventing them from doing so.

Creating an environment where effective cocreation is undertaken requires **psychological safety**. The educator is charged with the responsibility to ensure that all members of the learning community feel psychologically safe to be vulnerable, open, and risk-taking. It encourages them to connect with others in an authentic way, and to push the boundaries of expectations of what is possible for them and for others as learners in the classroom. Cocreating learning can only be effectively achieved if the environment holds a safe space for learners to be curious, to explore, and to engage with ideas in a reflective and critical way. Educaring from the heart requires both educators and learners to come to the classroom in an authentic and genuine way. It is the responsibility of the educator to ensure that they hold a space where children/young people can be open and be themselves without fear of failure or negative interactions, which could possibly undermine their confidence or courage in engaging in an authentic way.

Educaring from the heart places **care, empathy, and compassion** at the core of the work of an educator. It is fundamental to all aspects of learning, most especially when building the relationships required to nurture an environment within which cocreation of learning can be undertaken and realized to its maximum potential. Adopting an approach that is embedded within this ethic of care, empathy, and compassion creates the conditions within which learners feel psychologically safe to take risks, engage with others in an authentic way that nurtures mutual respect, and facilitates the multidirectional dialogue required within a cocreative learning environment. Creativity flourishes when individuals feel safe. Adopting an approach embedded with care, empathy, and compassion contributes positively to that sense of safety and confidence to take risks in/through the cocreative process. At a very fundamental level, it also allows for children/young people to feel seen and heard, instilling in them a sense of care, empathy, and compassion as they experience it directly for themselves. As such, it creates a ripple impact, teaching pupils/students about the importance of care, empathy, and compassion in their own lives, and within our broader societies. Cocreating education provides an opportunity to teach about the importance of care, empathy, and compassion in an increasingly complex and fractured globalized society.

The cocreative learning environment is **dynamic and responsive**, characterized by a sense of busyness, productivity, and noise. There is an energy to cocreation as members of a learning community build relationships, connect, and explore their learning. This energy can manifest in physical, spiritual, and emotional ways. Cocreative learning is expressed physically through noise, body language, movement, and flow as learners respond to the interactions in the classroom. It can also be physically expressed through the products of the cocreative process, such as projects and written or creative artefacts. Spiritual expressions of cocreation emerge through the deeply relational aspects of learning in this way. It can be a soulful experience, nurturing the spiritual aspects of how learners understand their humanity and place in the world. Such spiritual expression of cocreation manifests through improved sense of wellbeing and contentment with self. This contributes positively to the emotional response to and from the cocreative process, enhancing self-confidence, self-belief, and a positive sense of self. Such positive psychosocial responses also contribute to enhanced learner identity and wellbeing in education.

Cocreating learning in a heart-full way promotes increased **engagement and enthusiasm** for both learner and educator. This leads to enhanced and more effective teaching and learning in the learning environment. Cocreating learning empowers learner autonomy, placing the locus of control for engagement with them, as well as the degree to which they choose to engage within the process. The relational and community-based approach to cocreation further distributes the learning across a group, with the responsibility for learning dispersed among learners. As such, the decision to engage is with the learner rather than the educator. This empowers the learner to make a conscious decision to engage with peers in and through the learning process, contributing to increased engagement, enthusiasm, and motivation for learning.

Cocreation means that **teaching and learning is multidirectional**, with the locus of pedagogical power moving between all members of the learning community at any one time. While the educator holds the pedagogic knowledge, competency, and skill to scaffold an environment within which creative pedagogy can be facilitated, the nature of the cocreative process means that the flow of curricular content moves between learner and educator, allowing for multidirectional teaching and learning. Such multidirectional movement does not serve to undermine the pedagogic expertise of the educator. To the contrary, it affords an opportunity for educators to push the boundaries of pedagogy beyond expectations, empowering a deeper and more meaningful democratic approach to engaging children/young people with their learning. Cocreating heart-full education positions educator and pupil/student as both learner and teacher within the learning community. This means that all knowledge offered to the cocreated learning community is equally valued. It also facilitates an enhanced democratic approach to learner-centred pedagogy, placing the child/young person at the heart of the learning process, realising their rights as active agents and citizens within their learning worlds, as recognized within the UN Convention on the Rights of the Child (UNCRC).

Educaring from the heart recognizes the importance and value of all contributions made by members of the learning community. As such, **all learner community contributions are equally valued** in/through/with the cocreation process. Valuing all contributions is a fundamental principle within the educaring from the heart framework, working to promote an enhanced and more equitable approach to empowering all voices in education. It takes confidence to use one's voice in the classroom, and as such the role of the educator is critical in creating a learning environment within which learners can take risks and share their voices in a safe space. This is especially important when encouraging children/young people to engage in blue-sky or out-of-the-box thinking, which can at times be perceived as incorrect or out of the ordinary. This building of learner confidence to be able to contribute to the learning community through the cocreative process arises from a sense that all contributions are welcomed and valued without negative judgement. The temporal aspects of building environments where learners have the confidence, freedom, and trust to feel comfortable taking risks and to share their ideas cannot be overstated. Trust builds over time, as does the ability to engage within the cocreative process in a meaningful way. The greater the time given to cocreation, the deeper and more meaningful the learning.

It is evident from the discussion throughout this book that educaring from the heart requires both learners and educators to take **risks and be vulnerable** when cocreating learning in the classroom. While the educator takes risks in redistributing the pedagogic power through the cocreative process, the learner must trust that the environment created is a safe space for them to engage in an open, authentic, and genuine way. This positions both educator and learner as vulnerable and, while the cocreative process may be scaffolded, the outcome from engaging within the learning community is largely unknown. Educaring from the heart encourages both educator and learner to task risks and be vulnerable, to nurture the conditions where all members can contribute equally to the cocreative process. Indeed, it can be argued that cocreation of learning cannot be undertaken in the absence of risk and vulnerability from all members of the community. Nurturing risk taking and vulnerability within our classrooms is especially important for modelling this approach to learners as active citizens in our communities, our societies, and in our increasingly complex world. It also provides a critical foundation to teaching empathy and compassion, a core principle of educaring from the heart, by acknowledging the position and circumstance of learners as a risk-taking and vulnerable 'other' within the learning environment.

Creativity and innovation are at the heart of the pedagogic encounter when engaging in/through/with cocreative learning communities. The role of creativity and innovation in and across our societies is increasingly important, particularly when faced with the complex challenges facing humanity in an ever-more interdependent and globalised world. Providing opportunities for our children and young people to develop the skills and competencies to engage in creative and innovative ways of thinking differently in addressing real-life challenges is garnering increasing attention, most especially across the field of education. Cocreating learning begins with recognizing that all members of a learning community are agents with the potential to directly impact and shape the world around them in creative ways. Creativity and innovation are closely intertwined, with innovation considered an outward expression of creativity in addressing a challenge or improving the world around us. Cocreative learning communities provide a safe space for learners to express their creativity in open and dynamic ways, encouraging new ways of thinking and being in the world around them, while also facilitating opportunities for children/young people to convey their creativity through innovative expressions (such as approaches, resources, physical artefacts, ideas, etc.). Educaring from the heart is a creative undertaking in education, supported by creativity and innovation, which works to transform how learners experience teaching, learning, and agency within education. It shapes new expectations for pedagogy that expand far beyond what is currently fathomable in our systems and societies.

Cocreation of learning through a heart-full approach also contributes strongly to the development of *critical-thinking skills* among learners. Critical thinking is an essential component for creativity and innovation through which learners are challenged to critically engage, reflect, and question challenges and issues, while also seeking creative and innovative solutions to problems. Deep engagement with critical thinking is realized when a learner is effectively engaged in/through/with pedagogy designed to encourage problem solving in creative and innovative ways. Learner trust is crucial to facilitate their ability to take risks, to engage critically with content when cocreating learning within a broader community of practice. Cocreating heart-full education nurtures positive learning environments within which children and young people can engage freely with critical thinking in a safe manner. Critical thinking skills are especially important as humanity faces complex challenges around climate change, war, migration, and energy crises, to name a few.

Educaring from the heart is a democratic approach to pedagogy that is **learner-centric**. It places the child/young person at the heart of the educational process. Adopting a heart-full approach to cocreating learning requires educators to put children/young people at the heart of the community of practice. Educators follow learner curiosity as the impetus for motivating the learning to be cocreated in the classroom. It is from this seed of curiosity that deep and meaningful learning can occur. Adopting this approach creates conditions for which the learner can bring their authentic self to the pedagogic encounter in the knowledge that the locus of power has been redistributed, while their ideas are equally valued in a nonjudgmental way. While the learner is actively placed at the heart of the learning process, the educator scaffolds the environment for a more democratic approach to pedagogy, which not only listens to learner voices but also acts upon the solutions and ideas shared by them in the cocreative process. Responding in a meaningful and heart-full way consolidates the positioning of learners as valued and active agents within the classroom environment. As such, they develop their sense of citizenship and autonomy, which empowers them to engage as active agents within their worlds, beyond the physical boundaries of our educational institutions. This is a key aspect to recognizing children and young people as active citizens within the world now rather than only preparing them for a role in the future.

The following reflective template (Table 10.2) is an invitation to consider your own practice to cocreating learning in the classroom. Are there opportunities for you, as educator, to create and/or adopt approaches that encourage cocreation in/through/with pedagogy in your own practice?

Cocreation of learning is fundamental to realizing heart-full education in and across our education systems. Educaring from the heart calls on educators to adopt this dynamic and democratic approach to learning to promote increased engagement, motivation, and agency among learners in the classroom, enabling their sense of autonomy and citizenship within the classroom and beyond into our wider societies. Cocreation of learning not only offers transformative possibilities for educator and learner, but it simultaneously affords our societies the opportunity to develop in empathic and compassionate ways to address complex social, cultural, economic, environmental, and political challenges in an increasingly complex, interdependent world. The next chapter further explores this journey as 'we' in engaging in creativity as an approach to enhancing wellbeing in our educational institutions, and across our societies.

Table 10.2 Opportunities to cocreate and lead heart-full learning

Opportunities to cocreate and lead heart-full learning What are the opportunities to cocreate and lead heart-full learning in your classroom? How can you realise these opportunities in your context and what do you need to facilitate cocreative learning under each of the characteristics listed below?

Sharing and rebalance/distribution of power	Engagement and enthusiasm
Mutual Respect	Multidirectional teaching and learning
Free expression and two-way dialogue	All community contributions equally valued
Movement and Flow	Risk and vulnerability
Psychological safety	Creativity and innovation
Care, empathy, and compassion	Critical-thinking skills
Dynamic and responsive	Learner-centric pedagogy

Educaring from the Heart

Capture your thoughts & feelings here

11 Creativity for Wellbeing

This penultimate chapter of *Educaring from the Heart* explores the role creativity plays in nurturing our wellbeing as educators, which in turn impacts the wellbeing of pupils/students in the learning context within which we are working. Within this perspective creativity is defined as the process of putting something new or novel into the world, ranging from ideas to physical artefacts, and encompasses everyday creativity as well as big-*C creativity* associated with arts-based approaches, such as art, drama, music, and so on. Contrary to common misunderstanding, creativity belongs to everyone. This means that everyone has the potential to be creative. It is a skill that can be taught rather than a gift that is received. Indeed, common misperceptions associated with creativity are that it only belongs to those who engage in arts-based approaches. However, as has been argued earlier in this book, creativity is a core aspect of educaring from the heart. It affords the opportunity for both educator and learner to engage with each other, and the world around them, in creative and novel ways to explore challenges, design solutions, and critically reflect on issues impacting humanity both in our local and global communities. Engaging children and young people in/through/with creative pedagogies develops their creative skills and competencies to enhance their ability to be agile and responsive to issues that impact their lives, as well as the lives of those living across the globe. This is especially important in cultivating a sense of global citizenship among children and young people as they seek to make sense of their identity and belonging in their local communities as well as in the world beyond.

There is increased international focus on the importance of nurturing wellbeing within and across education systems. Indeed, educational institutions are increasingly engaging with policy and practice to support both the wellbeing of educator and learner across education systems. This increased focus on wellbeing in education has resulted in a paradoxical positioning of wellbeing as an add-on approach in education, with additional time being ringfenced for curricular content purposefully aimed at enhancing wellbeing in education. However, more challenging for

DOI: 10.4324/9781032718194-14

educators is the embedding of wellbeing into pedagogy as an effective approach to the everyday interactions within the learning environment. Embedding wellbeing into pedagogy is essential to realizing enhanced wellbeing within and across our educational communities. This is especially true in environments where there has traditionally been a distance between educator and pupil/student (such as in the large lecture theatres of higher educational institutions). Educaring from the heart provides a framework within which educators can embed wellbeing in/through/ with pedagogy when collaborating with pupils/students to cocreate learning in the classroom.

Creativity and wellbeing are inextricably linked. While creativity can enhance wellbeing, it is not necessary to have a positive sense of wellbeing to be creative. Indeed, creativity can also arise in times when an individual is experiencing a negative sense of wellbeing. The process of engaging creatively can enhance wellbeing, particularly when working as a community of learners in the classroom. Wellbeing within this context is cumulative. Time, space, and relationships play a critical role in the enhancing creative wellbeing in education (Figure 11.1).

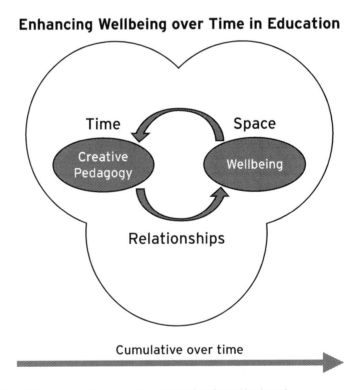

Figure 11.1 Creativity and wellbeing when educaring from the heart

Time is a critical aspect when nurturing wellbeing through pedagogy. Educators and learners need adequate time to engage in/though/with creative pedagogy. As such, it is critical that educational policy promotes the importance of allocating time to creative pedagogies in the classroom to promote the wellbeing of both educators and learners. Time is a resource that can be sparse in education. As such, it is important that educators reflect on alternative approaches to embedding creativity into the everyday work in the classroom. The first step is recognizing that all educators are/can be creative regardless of the subject being taught or their background/experience with creativity. Moving to embed creativity into existing practices is the most effective way to find time to engage with creative pedagogy in education systems, which are already under time pressures and constraints.

Spaces to enable creativity are especially important when seeking to enhance wellbeing through creative practices. The physical spaces in our educational institutions can either serve to enable or restrict effective creative practices between educators and learners. Physical space is a premium resource within educational institutions, often under pressure in terms of the nature of usage, the capacity of children/young people in the space, the furniture and resources available for use, and the flexibility to adapt to meet the requirements of engaging in/through/with creative pedagogy. Such requirements include, but are not limited to, issues relating to flexibility regarding how the space is set up and used, capacity to move around and explore in cocreative ways, furniture to enable creativity (such as creating circles rather than working in linear rows), movement and flow to move freely within the learning environment, and resources to engage leaners in/through/with creative pedagogy. It is also important to note that creative pedagogy can also be employed outside of the physical boundaries of fixed learning environments or classrooms, such as in nature, the wider communities within which educational institutions are located, and in the informal in-between spaces of education.

Creativity and wellbeing are predominantly negotiated in/through/with relationships when cocreating learning in the learning environment using the educaring from the heart approach. Within this perspective, relationships play a critical role in translating creativity into wellbeing, and indeed, wellbeing into creativity. Creative practices and pedagogy can contribute directly to the enhancement of both the educator's and learner's wellbeing within the learning environment, especially when working together as a community of learners.

There are two key aspects to building these creative relationships. The first relates to opportunity to engage in creative ways. The environment within which creative relationships are facilitated and nurtured is especially important to enhancing wellbeing through creativity. The role of educator is to provide the optimum environment within which these creative relationships can be established and nurtured over time. This then contributes to the second aspect of building creative relationships: ensuring a depth and authenticity to the nature of the relationships that are formed. High-quality relationships established and nurtured within the learning environment can contribute positively to wellbeing as negotiated through creative pedagogy with learners. It is also important to note that both learner and educator benefit from enhanced wellbeing through creative pedagogy. The EDUCARE principles for wellbeing in/through/with creativity provide a guide to educators for putting this into practice (Figure 11.2).

The creative environment needs to be ***welcoming*** to contribute to the enhancement of learner and educator wellbeing. Educators are charged with the responsibility of creating welcoming environments within which both learner and educator can engage in an open way. Welcoming learning environments provide safe spaces for curiosity and creativity through collaboration, enhancing the quality of relationships within a learning community and contributing to positive individual and collective wellbeing. Creating safe spaces for creative learning also ensures an ***engaging*** environment within which learners are immersed in experiential-learning encounters, while also being valued as key contributors to the learning process. As

EDUCARE Principles for wellbeing in/through/with creativity

Welcoming

Engaging

Linking & Connecting

Lively & Dynamic

Brave & Bold

Enriching

Inclusive

Nurturing

Genuine

Figure 11.2 EDUCARE principles for wellbeing in/through/with creativity

such, engagement in/through/with creativity can enhance wellbeing. This is most evident when **linking and connecting** children and young people to curricular content and other members of the learning community, including peers and educators. It is through shared creative experiences and deep relational connection that wellbeing is enhanced for all members of the learning community.

Cocreative learning environments are **lively and dynamic**. They express energy and enthusiasm and are experienced as fun and joyful. Evoking positive feelings of affect can only contribute positively to wellbeing, particularly when the environment supports playful and compelling learning. Engaging in the cocreative learning environment requires both learners and educators to be **brave and bold**. While the educator has be brave in redistributing pedagogic power across the learning community, the learner must be bold, take risks, and engage in a genuine and authentic way. As a result, the cocreative environment is **enriching** in terms of socioemotional and academic development, contributing to an enhanced sense of self and wellbeing. Cocreation within a learning community reinforces a strengths-based approach to education, where each member of the community is valued equally through this **inclusive** pedagogical practice. Being seen and accepted for who you are in education is one of the most powerful experiences for learners, and adopting cocreation provides safe spaces where all members of a community are included in a meaningful way, contributing to enhanced wellbeing for all. To enhance wellbeing through creativity it is critical to embed values of care, empathy, and compassion within this approach. These are the fundamental principles underpinning educaring from the heart, which seeks to create **nurturing** learning environments through which wellbeing for all can be enhanced. Children and young people thrive when they feel cared about and for, and as educators we play a key role in ensuring they experience such care within and across our education systems. Finally, when enhancing wellbeing through creativity, both educators and learners are expected to engage in **genuine** and authentic ways. It is through genuine connection and engagement that creative pedagogy is realized, and positive relationships are nurtured, enhancing wellbeing for all members of the learning community.

This chapter has argued that creativity realized through co-creation can contribute positively to enhancing wellbeing for all in our learning communities. The next exercise is an invitation to consider how best to nurture your student/pupil wellbeing through creative pedagogy in your classroom (Table 11.1).

This chapter has explored the role of creativity and cocreation for nurturing wellbeing in education. Educaring from the heart requires educators to adopt a heart-full approach with learners, nurturing their wellbeing and sense of belonging in education and beyond. The final chapter presents the overarching framework for educaring from the heart to empower educators to embed care, empathy, and care at the heart of their work in education.

Table 11.1 Exercise: Nurturing wellbeing through creative pedagogy

---

Nurturing Wellbeing through Creative Pedagogy in the Learning Environment
Take a moment to reflect, under each of the headings below, on the opportunities to nurture wellbeing in your learning context through creative practices.

Welcoming: How do/can you creative a welcoming environment to encourage creative practices in your context?

Engaging: How can you enhance pupil/student engagement in your environment through creative practice?

Linking and connecting: How can you enhance learner experience of linking and connecting to (a) curricular content and (b) each other, to build relationships in your context?

Lively and dynamic: How can you ensure your pupils/students are engaging in a lively and dynamic way when engaging in learning?

Brave and bold: How can you enhance the learning environment so that all members of the community can be vulnerable and take risks through the creative process?

Enriching: How can you ensure that teaching and learning is enriching all learners, both socioemotionally and academically?

Inclusive: How can the approach to teaching using cocreative practices to enhance inclusion in your context?

Nurturing: How can pupil/student wellbeing be nurture through creative pedagogy and cocreation in the learning environment?

Genuine: How can the conditions within the learning environment be enhanced to facilitate children/young people to engage in genuine and authentic ways?

Educaring from the Heart

Capture your thoughts & feelings here

Part 4: Uniting "I", "We", and "Us" - A Framework for Educaring from the Heart

12 A Framework for Educaring from the Heart

This final chapter presents the overarching framework for educaring from the heart, drawing on the key principles and values presented throughout this book. The purpose of this framework is to provide a scaffold upon which educators can shape their educaring practice in and across the education system. This framework is intended to inform and inspire practice rather than prescribe overly specific, reductionist 'to-dos' to realise this approach in our educational institutions. This is to recognize the professionalism, autonomy, and agency of educators as skilled and competent pedagogues across our education system. In drawing together the "I", "We", and "Us" in this chapter, each of which are key components of the pedagogic encounter, the holistic nature of who you are as an educator is recognized. This uniting of these three aspects of who we are, how we are defined, and how we define ourselves plays an integral role in shaping who we are and how we engage as agents for educare in education. While the three sections of this book have unpacked these three components, this chapter reflects on how these reunite and inform our approach to pedagogic practice with learners (Figure 12.1).

Educaring from the heart starts with recognizing the complexities of who we are and how we understand ourselves as educators. We carry these complexities with us in our pedagogic a metaphorical backpack. This educator backpack is fundamental in shaping the lens through which we see and understand the learners we work with in our contexts, whether early childhood settings, schools, or higher education institutions. Identifying and recognizing the different parts of who we are helps us better understand why we approach our work and interact with learners in the way we do. Reflecting on our educator backpack can help guide us in identifying positive aspects of ourselves that we bring to the pedagogic encounter, while also affording us an opportunity to reflect on improvements we could make in our everyday interaction in the learning environment. It is not often in education we are invited to step back and deeply consider and reflect on those aspects of

DOI: 10.4324/9781032718194-16

Uniting the 'I', 'We' and 'Us' through the Pedagogic Encounter

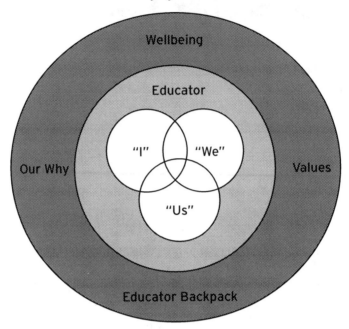

Figure 12.1 Reuniting "I", "We", and "Us" – the educare educator

ourselves we bring into that pedagogic encounter. The educator backpack provides a tool to help guide us through such a process.

The complexity of who we are and what we bring into the learning environment is also shaped by our values. These values shape who we are as educators and how we approach different aspects of our practices with our learners. As such, it is important to reflect on our values and whether and how they are shaping our practice as educators in the learning environment. Querying if and how we bring our values to our educational context helps us better understand the approaches we are taking with our students, allowing us to better understand whether our work with learners aligns with our core values, as individuals and as educators. It is important to consider whether there is alignment or divergence between our individual values and those we hold as educators, as well as whether this alignment or divergence impacts how we perceive and approach our work with learners. Educaring from the heart invites educators to take a values-based approach to working with children and young people, placing care, empathy, and compassion at the heart of pedagogic encounter.

Working in education is intensive and it is challenging to find time to reflect on our *why*. Indeed, it is not often educators are invited to consider their *why*, which is a vital aspect for our motivation in our work and the nature of our engagement with our pupils/students. Educaring from the heart invites educators to reflect on their *why* to rediscover their purpose and value in education. Rediscovering and reminding yourself of your purpose in education is important in sustaining your engagement, energy, and motivation in your work. As educators, we give a lot of ourselves all the time, including physically, emotionally, mentally, spiritually, and often we do not have the opportunity to restore our energy as we engage in our daily work. Reminding ourselves of our *why* becomes an important tool for sustaining ourselves and our motivation in education.

The constant giving of ourselves impacts our wellbeing as educators. Educaring from the heart invites educators to invest time in nurturing their wellbeing to ensure that they can continue to sustain themselves and their motivation when working with learners in education. Educators work beyond the technical and skillful competencies of delivering curriculum. They also engage in the moment-to-moment complexities of the relational dynamics within the learning environment. Navigating such complexities while delivering curriculum is complex, drawing especially on the educator's emotional and relational energy. This invisible work within the learning environment impacts educator wellbeing both positively and negatively. Of particular importance is the opportunity for educators to nurture their wellbeing, especially when they are feeling depleted or lack the emotional energy required to give to their pupils/students. However, the intensification of time in education has resulted in a deterioration of opportunities for educators to restore their wellbeing. Nurturing educator wellbeing is critical to nurturing the wellbeing of our child/youth in education. Educaring from the heart invites educators to identify opportunities to enhance their wellbeing using tools to guide them. A crisis in educator wellbeing is a crisis in learner wellbeing, and it is incumbent upon education systems to act to ensure that there is adequate time, space, and resources to enhance the wellbeing of all in education. Doing so will ensuring a healthier, more empathic, and compassionate society for everyone.

Educaring from the heart brought us through a journey from individual educator into a community of learning, which is reflected in the sections starting with "I" (educator), "We" (relational pedagogy), and "Us" (learning community). Unpacking each of these layers provided an opportunity to place the educator at the heart of the work in education ("I"), and then reflecting on relational complexities as we move from individual to partnership ("We" – educator and learner) through to community ("Us" – cocreative learning). It is within and between the spaces of these layers that both educators and learners navigate the educational process. Recognising and understanding the complexity and nuances of each layer is vital if we are truly to understand who we are and what we do as educators in and across education systems. Educaring from the heart provides a framework for understanding our practice as educators and for guiding our educational journey

A Framework for Educaring from the Heart

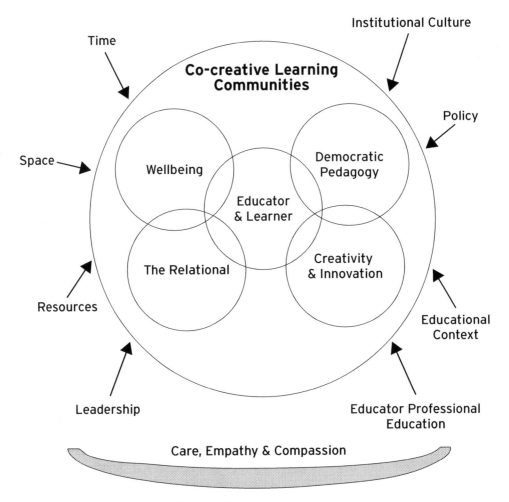

Figure 12.2 A Framework for educaring from the heart

onward, placing particular emphasis on care, empathy, and compassion at the heart of our work (Figure 12.2).

Educaring from the heart places the educator and learner at the heart of the framework to indicate their centrality at the heart of the education system. Caring for our educators and learners is critical to ensure we have an effective and healthy education system that serves our wider communities and societies. Educaring from the heart recognizes the transformative possibilities of caring for educators and learners, and for modelling and nurturing care, empathy, and compassion, which ripple out into our broader societies, making real impact and changing the lives of those in our world.

The four key pillars within this framework are wellbeing, relational pedagogy, democratic pedagogy, and creativity and innovation. Educaring from the heart emphasizes the importance of both educator and learner ***wellbeing*** to ensure effective engagement and learning in our education systems. It offers tools for considering how best to nurture both educator and learner wellbeing, while also considering strategies and approaches to embedding wellbeing in/through/with pedagogy in the classroom. The complexity and power of ***relational pedagogy*** aspects of our work as educators is also critical to explore when considering how to approach educaring from the heart. Relational pedagogy is the cornerstone upon which education is realized. Indeed, education cannot be undertaken effectively in the absence of positive relationships. As such, relational pedagogy plays a critical role in educaring from the heart, where meaningful, authentic, and genuine relationships contribute to creating a care-full, empathic, and compassionate learning environment within which learners can come as their authentic selves to engage as a valued member of a wider learning community.

Placing children/young people at the heart of the pedagogic encounter is a key aspect of the learning process when educaring from the heart. Redistributing the pedagogic power from educator to learner creates opportunities to engage in a more child-rights based ***democratic pedagogy***, which both facilitates and responds to child/youth voices, allowing them to engage now as active agents and citizens of the world in rather than in preparation for the future. ***Creativity and innovation*** facilitate an environment within which children and young people can explore ideas, engage in critical thinking, and design solutions for challenges they identify as impacting their worlds. Creative pedagogy proffers opportunities to adopt a more democratic approach to teaching and learning while also enhancing the wellbeing of all members within the learning community.

These four pillars of wellbeing, relational pedagogy, democratic pedagogy, and creativity and innovation are situated within the broader context of the learning environment, conceptualized within the educaring from the heart framework as cocreative learning communities. These learning communities come together to explore the world with curiosity and critical thinking to empathise with and understand the complexities of challenges and problems facing an increasing interdependent world. The transformative power of embedding care, empathy, and compassion at the heart of these learning communities is profound, particularly as learners move between the formal spaces of education and the wider informal spaces of their worlds and the world around them. Working in partnership with others as a valued member of a learning community places emphasis on a strengths-based approach to teaching and learning, one in which the learner is an expert explorer and educator is an expert guide. This journey of exploration in/through/with creative and democratic pedagogy led by children/young people contributes to enhanced and more authentic relationships, deeper and more meaningful learning, and improved collective and individual wellbeing.

Educaring from the heart invites educators to understand and recognize their importance and how critical their work is in contributing not only to the development of individuals, but also in shaping the communities and worlds outside of our educational institutions. However, it is also important to recognize the external factors that can influence and work to either enable or prevent educators from reaching the aspirations for educaring from the heart. Educator autonomy and agency is critical to ensuring their professionalism and expertise is supported within education. However, there are limits to the degree of agency afforded to educators, and as such there can be frustration between what is expected and what can be realistically achieved in education. The external factors that can work to either enable or prevent educators in educaring from the heart include time, space, resources, leadership, educator professional education, educational context, policy, and institutional culture.

Perhaps one of the most important resources for ensuring educators can meaningfully and effectively adopt care, empathy, and compassion into their practice is **time**. However, in an increasingly intensified educational landscape, time is in short supply with educators who are under pressure to deliver more while also managing the complexity of learner needs in the classroom. However, supplying educators with time to invest in caring for themselves and for their pupils/students can only pay dividends, contributing to enhanced engagement in education, improved wellbeing and a sense of belonging, identification of challenges for early intervention, and deeper, more meaningful relationships within the learning environment.

Space is also a resource often under pressure within and across education systems, yet it is an important facilitator for educaring from the heart. The physical spaces in our education systems either serve to prevent or facilitate a care-full approach with learners. Creating welcoming spaces that are flexible rather than fixed, which allow for movement and flow and have enough capacity for all learners to explore, learning freely – these kinds of spaces afford optimum conditions when educaring from the heart. It is also possible to consider using the spaces outside of the more formal learning environment, such as going out into nature or into the local community. Creating spaces that nurture relationships and provide opportunities to connect with others through the learning process is key to taking a heart-full approach to teaching and learning.

Educators and learners also require adequate **resources** when educaring from the heart. Such resources should enable learners to engage with learning with curiosity and creativity, drawing on a variety of approaches and supplies. Having free choice and opportunity to engage with a depth and range of resources allows learners to lead their learning without barriers interrupting their creativity and critical thinking. Resources can range from digitally based approaches to physical materials that facilitate the learning journey for each pupil/student. Resources can also provide an opportunity for those within the learning community to make deep connections, enhancing wellbeing and engagement in learning.

Leadership is fundamental when educaring from the heart, powerfully influencing the possibilities and opportunities for both educators and learners to engage in this heart-full approach to education. While educators play a key leadership role in facilitating learning environments that are embedded in care, empathy and compassion, the role of leadership within educational institutions cannot be underestimated. To engage in educaring requires that educators and learners be supported and encouraged by visionary leadership that recognizes the value and significance of adopting this approach in the learning environment. Educaring from the heart also contributes directly to the development of leadership skills and competencies for children and young people as they engage in a more democratic approach to learning.

Educator professional education across the educational continuum from early childhood through to higher education plays a key role in developing skills, competencies, and confidence in adopting a care-full, empathic, and compassionate approach with learners. It is critical that curriculum content within educator professional education programmes, from initial engagement through to continuous professional development, focuses on nurturing the pedagogic skills required to facilitate an educaring from the heart approach in learning environments. These skills require educators to build deep and meaningful relationships, nurture wellbeing for themselves and learners, facilitate a democratic approach to teaching and learning, and embed creativity and innovation into the learning process. Furthermore, it requires that educators understand and value the prioirtising of care, empathy, and compassion within and across our education systems. Educating our educators is fundamental to realising the vision of educaring from the heart.

The **educational context** within which the learning environment is located directly shapes the educators' approach when educaring from the heart. Educator engagement with this framework will vary when working with young children in early childhood contexts, or when engaging with pupils and students in primary and post-primary/secondary schools, while also differing when working with individuals in higher and further education. However, the four core pillars supporting the educaring from the heart approach provide the scaffolding upon which the framework can be adapted to reflect the relevant educational context. The ethics of care, empathy, and compassion provides a value-based compass upon which the interactions within the cocreative learning community engage and relate across the continuum of education. While the educational demands on students increase at the upper end of the educational continuum, sometimes at the expense of more democratic and creative pedagogy, it is within these contexts where increased focus on adopting this educaring from the heart framework has potential to be most impactful for all members of the learning community.

Education policy, set at international and national levels, filters down to directly impact and shape pedagogic practices in and across respective learning context and environments. This is especially the case in situations where education policy is reviewed and assessed as part of an evaluative process. Curricular policy has a profound impact on what is taught and how it is taught in our education settings. Assessment, when present, attributes higher status to what is considered valuable knowledge within curricular content. As such, a tension can emerge between engaging learners in/through educational processes and preparing learners for assessment/measurement for educational outcomes. This tension between process and outcome can indirectly influence and constrain educator agency in engaging learners in more experiential and democratically informed pedagogic approaches. When educaring from the heart, it is critical to problematize and question such tensions, while also inviting educators to be brave and take risks in pushing the boundaries of pedagogic expectations when working with learners.

The **educational institutional culture** has a profound influence on our work as educators. An educational culture that supports agency, creativity, innovation, curiosity, exploration, community, and measured risk taking to push boundaries contributes to the flourishing of educaring from the heart. If a culture is averse to creative and innovative approaches to teaching and learning, it can indirectly prevent learners from engaging in more deep, meaningful and connected teaching and learning. It also limits the opportunities for children and young people to develop skills and competencies that are essential to engaging challenges in responsive and dynamic ways. Educaring from the heart provides a framework for scaffolding pedagogic approaches that are fundamental to developing the skills required to address the challenges facing humanity in a care-full, empathic, and compassionate way. It creates an environment in which learners can explore and understand who they are and how they understand those around them, nurturing a culture of belonging and wellbeing. Creating positive cultures for children and young people to thrive and flourish is fundamental to educaring from the heart.

Educaring from the heart aspires for both educators and learners to engage one another through an ethics of **care, empathy, and compassion**. The transformative possibilities for educators, learners, and our wider society in taking this approach in education has been discussed throughout this book. It is critical not to lose sight of the important role educators and education systems play in contributing to more care-full, empathic, and compassionate societies. Educaring from the heart proffers a framework to guide educators, policy makers, and those working within and across education to refocus their attention on building heart-full societies that can challenge the complexities and challenges facing humanity – and ultimately change the world. Perhaps there is no greater purpose than that for education.

Educaring from the Heart

Capture your thoughts & feelings here

Index

Note: For figure citations, page numbers appear in *italics*. For table citations, page numbers appear in **bold**.

abuse 41

acceptance *68, 69, 70*, 87, 88, *90*

accessibility *68, 69, 70*

accountability 83

administrative paperwork 83

affirmation *68, 69, 70*

Aked, J. 53

arts-based approaches 115; *see also* creativity

aspirations: dreams and 71, *72, 73*

authentic and genuine interaction *68, 69, 70*

authenticity 87, 88, *90*

backpacks *see* educator backpack, invisible knapsack

blue-sky thinking 110

body language *17*, 18, 109

brain development 11, 12

burnout 13, 49, 81

care 51, 76-9; caring for *vs.* caring about 76, *77*; cocreative learning environment **106**, 108-9, **113**; compassionate education 76; creative wellbeing and 119; definition of 76; educaring from the heart care audit *84*; empathy and compassion, interaction with *3, 77, 81*; ethics of 108, 131-2; psychologically safe learning environment *68, 69, 70*

career opportunities *39*, 40

childcare responsibilities 14

childhood 10, *10*, 12, 27; development 11, 12; early childhood settings 4, 40, 50, 125, 131; family of origin 11; positive experiences 11

citizenship 2, 51, 76, 92, 101, 112, 115

classroom: dynamics *39*, 41; resources 41; volatility 41, 78

climate change 2, 37, 78, 112

coaching 14

cocreative learning environment 105, **106**, 108, **113**, 127, 129, 131; creativity and innovation 111; dynamic and responsive 109; lively and dynamic 119; *see also* heart-full education

collaborative approach 93, 95, 101

communities of practice 55

community *39*, 40-1, *43*; contributions, equal value of **106**, 110, **113**

compassion 78-81; care and empathy, interaction with *3, 81*; cocreative learning environment **106**, 108-9, **113**; creative wellbeing and 119; definition of 78; EDUCARE principles 87, 88, *90*; ethics of 108, 131-2; psychologically safe learning environment *68, 69, 70*; *see also* compassionate education

compassionate education 76-85; apply *78, 79*; dialogue *78, 79*; identify *78, 79*; importance of 81; reflection on compassionate approach *80*; respond *78, 79*; sustain *78, 79*; *see also* compassion

connection 87, 88, *90*

constructive feedback *68, 69, 70*

Cordon, C. 53

creativity *17*, 115-21, *128*, 129; bold *118*, **120**; brave *118*, **120**; connecting *118*, **120**; cocreative learning environment **106**, 111, **113**; creative being *72, 73*; dynamic *118*, **120**;

EDUCARE principles *118*, 118-20; engaging *118*, 118-19, **120**; Enhancing Wellbeing over Time in Education *116*; enriching *118*, 119, **120**; genuine *118*, 119, **120**; inclusive *118*, 119, **120**; linking *118*, **120**; lively *118*, **120**; nurturing *118*, 119, **120**; welcoming 118, *118*, **120**

critical thinking skills **106**, 111-12, **113**

cultural background 25

cultural worlds 10, 11-2

curiosity *17*, 87, *87*, *90*

curriculum and assessment *39*

delight 87, *87*, *90*

democracy 18

democratic pedagogy *128*, 129

dialogue: EDUCARE principles 86, *87*, *90*; mutual 106-7; two-way **106**, **113**

digital technologies 2, 81

dis/ability 25, 41, 51, 89, 94

domains of holistic education 16-21; emotional domain 16, *17*, *21*; philosophical domain *17*, 18-9, *21*; physical domain 16-8, *17*, *21*; relational domain *17*, 19, *21*; skilful domain *17*, 18, *21*; spiritual domain *17*, 19-20, *21*

dynamic environment **106**, 109, **113**

early childhood education 40

EDUCARE principles 86-90; acceptance *87*, 88, *90*; authenticity *87*, 88, *90*; compassion *87*, 88, *90*; connection *87*, 88, *90*; creative wellbeing *118*, 118-20; curiosity 87, *87*, *90*; delight 87, *87*, *90*; dialogue 86, *87*, *90*; empathy 87-8, *87*, *90*; engagement 86, *87*, *90*; equity *87*, 89, *90*; inclusion *87*, 89, *90*; personal reflection *90*; relational principles *87*, 89; respect *87*, 88, *90*; trust *87*, 88, *90*; understanding 87-8, *87*, *90*; voice(s) *93*, 93-5

education policy 132

education system 37, *39*, 39-40, *43*; cultural influences 39; partnership 39; psychological basis 39; public engagement 39; social purpose 39; sociological basis 39

educational context 131

educational experiences 10, *10*, 14

educational institutional culture 132

educational opportunities 10, *10*, 14

educational psychologists 83

educator backpack 9-21, 25, 125-6

educator identity 9, *17*

educator professional education *128*, 130-1

educator toolkit *17*

emotion: emotional awareness 16, *17*; emotional domain 16, *17*, *21*; *see also* domains of holistic education

emotional experiences *17*

emotional literacy *17*

emotional maturity *17*

emotional responsiveness *68*, 69, *70*

emotional wellbeing *17*

empathy 51, 77-9; care and compassion, interaction with *3*, *80*; cocreative learning environment **106**, 108-9, **113**; creative wellbeing and 119; definition of 2, 77; EDUCARE principles 87-8, *87*, *90*; ethics of 108, 131-2; psychologically safe learning environment 68, 69, *70*

empowerment 2; pedagogy **97**; voice(s) 92-102

enacted approach 93, 95

energy crises 2, 112

engagement *33*, 34, *42*; barriers and opportunities *36*; cocreative learning environment **106**, 109; contextual factors *39*, *43*; EDUCARE principles 86, *87*, *90*

enthusiasm **106**, 109

equity 18, *87*, 89, *90*

ethical framework *17*, 19, 108, 131-2

ethnicity 25, 41, 51, 89, 94

family: circumstances 10, *10*, 14; composition 14; definitions of 14; experiences 11; of origin 10, 11, 14

feelings 2; *see also* emotion

Five Ways to Wellbeing framework 53-7; 'be active' 53, 55, **57**; 'connect' 53, 55, *55*, **57**; dandelion exercise *54*; 'give' 53, 56, **57**; 'keep learning' 53, 56, **57**; six pillars of educator wellbeing 55, 56; 'step back and step out' 53, 56, **57**; 'take notice' 53, 55, **57**

food crises 2

framework for educaring from the heart 125-33, *128*

free expression **106**, 106-7, **113**

Froebel approach 18

gender 41, 51, 89, 94; identity 25
grounded presence *17*

health 10, *10*, 13-4; *see also* wellbeing
heart-full education 105-14, 130; all learner
   community contributions, equal value of
   106, 110, **113**; care **106**, 108-9, **113**; cocreative
   learning environment, characteristics of **106**,
   107; compassion **106**, 108-9, **113**; creativity **106**,
   111, **113**; critical thinking skills **106**, 111-12, **113**;
   dialogue **106**, **113**; dynamic environment **106**,
   109, **113**; empathy **106**, 108-9, **113**; engagement
   106, 109; enthusiasm **106**, 109; free expression
   106, 106-7, **113**; innovation **106**, 111, **113**; learner-
   centric pedagogy **106**, 112, **113**; movement and
   flow **106**, 107, **113**; multidirectional learning
   and teaching **106**, 109-10, **113**; mutual dialogue
   106-7; mutual respect 106, **113**; opportunities
   to cocreate and lead heart-full learning **113**;
   power matrix *107*; power sharing 105-6;
   psychological safety **106**, 108, **113**; rebalancing
   power 105-6; redistribution of power 105-6;
   responsive environment **106**, 109, **113**; risk **106**,
   110-11, **113**; spiritual cocreation 109; vulnerability
   106, 110-11, **113**
hearts 71, *72*
hierarchy of needs 12
holistic development 2

inclusion 18, *87*, 89, *90*
inclusive approach *93*, 94-5, 101
Initial Teacher Education 4
innovation 129; cocreative learning environment
   106, 111, **113**
institutional culture 42, *128*, 132
institutional systems *39*, 40, *43*
intentional inclusion 68, 69, *70*
introspection *17*, 19
invisible knapsack: concept of 9-10

leadership 42, *128*, 130-1
learner-centric pedagogy **106**, 112, **113**
life journey *72*, 73
lifelong learning 56
literacy 37
Lundy, L.: model of participation 92-3

macroinfluences 37, *39*, *43*
Marks, N. 53
Maslow, A. H.: hierarchy of needs 12
maternalistic approach 13
McIntosh, P. 9
meaningful connection *17*
mental health 46-7; support 53
mentoring 14
migration 2, 37, 112
mindfulness **57**
misinformation 81
Montessori approach 18
motivation in education 4, *5*, 20, *33*, 34, *38*,
   42, 127; extrinsic motivation 36-7; intrinsic
   motivation 36-7
movement *17*; flow and **106**, 107, **113**
multidirectional learning and teaching **106**,
   109-10, **113**

national policy priorities *39*, 40
needs 71, *72*; hierarchy of 12
neoliberalism 2, 37, 40, 45
neurodiversity 47
New Economics Foundation 53
numeracy 37
nurturing in education 65-75, 127; creative
   wellbeing *118*, 119, **120**; identifying ways to
   nurture *74*

occupational psychologists 83
open dialogue 68, 69, 70
openhearted approach *93*, 94, 101
Organisation for Economic Co-operation and
   Development (OECD) 37
'out-of-the-box' thinking 110

participation: Lundy's model of *93*; voice(s) 96,
   101
partnership 68, 69, *70*
peer affiliation *see* positive peer affiliation
performativity drivers *39*, 41
personal relationships 10, *10*, 12-3
philosophical domain *17*, 18-9, *21*; *see also*
   domains of holistic education
physical domain 16-8, *17*, *21*; *see also* domains of
   holistic education

physical safety *68*, 69, *70*
physical space *see* space
physical wellbeing *17*
place *48*, 50
policy *128*; education 132; initiatives 27;
    international policymaking 37; voice(s) 96, 98,
    101
positive peer affiliation 68, *68*, *70*
positive relationships 68, *70*; safe learning
    environment 68
poverty 41
power: hegemonic distribution of 1; matrix of *107*;
    rebalancing 105-6; redistribution of 105-6;
    sharing 105-6
practices in education 96, 98, 101
productivity 49
professional development *39*, 49, 83; continuous
    17, 18
professional experiences 10, *10*, 15
professional identity 4, *17*, 18
professional relationships 10, *10*, 12-3
professional trust 42
psychological development 11
psychological responses: 'fight, flight, fawn, or
    freeze' 45-6, **46**
psychological safety 66, *66*, 67, 88; cocreative
    learning environment **106**, 108, **113**; safe
    learning environment 68; safety audit *70*
public engagement 39
public opinion 39-4, *39*
purpose in education 32-44, 65, 126-7;
    engagement and motivation 33; identifying *35*;
    purpose of education 37, 39

race 51, 89
re/formational spheres *10*
reflective practice *17*, 20
reflexity 69
relational domain *17*, 19, *21*; *see also* domains of
    holistic education
relational dynamics 27
relational pedagogy 86-91, 127, 129
relational principles *87*, 89
relationships: positive and thriving *17*, 19; *see
    also* personal relationships; professional
    relationships

representation *68*, 69, *70*
resources *128*, 130-1
respect *87*, 88, *90*, 106, **113**
responsive environment **106**, 109, **113**
risk taking 66, *66*, 71, **106**, 110-11, **113**

safe spaces *17*; *see also* psychological safety
self: authentic *17*, 19, 25, 27, *30*; care *17*; educator
    30; embodied sense of *17*; expression of *17*;
    professional *17*, 19; spiritual *72*, *73*; spiritual
    sense of *17*
sense-making *17*
sexual identity 89
sexual orientation 25
signposting practices *17*
skilful domain *17*, 18, *21*; *see also* domains of
    holistic education
social class 41, 51, 94
social media 81-2
social worlds 10, *10*, 13
socioeconomic factors: circumstances 25, *39*;
    disadvantage 14, 41; influences 10, *10*, 14-5, 27;
    perspectives 15; status 15, 89
socioemotional development 11, 13, 41, 119, **120**
sociohistorical contexts 14, 37
space *128*, 130; creative wellbeing and 117;
    importance of 93; physical 96-8, 101, 117; policy
    and practice *48*, 50; relational wellbeing and
    48, 50; representation and 50; safe 118; *see
    also* psychological safety
speech and language therapists 83
spiritual: cocreation 109; compass *17*;
    contribution *17*; domain *17*, 19-20, *21*;
    foundation stone *17*; purpose and vision *17*; self
    72, *73*; *see also* domains of holistic education
stakeholder agenda *39*
stress 45-7
student centred approach *17*; student needs 39
support 68, 69, *70*; voice(s) *93*, 95, 101

Thompson, S. 53
time *128*, 130; constraints 45; consumption
    of 81; creative wellbeing and *116*, 116-17;
    demands of *48*, 49; devaluation of *48*, 49-50;
    intensification of *48*, 49, 81, 83, 127; structure
    and 49

toxic culture 45

trauma 41; responses 45-6, **46**

trust 68, *68*, *70*, *87*, 88, *90*; *see also* professional trust

understanding 87-8, *87*, *90*

United Nations Convention on the Rights of the Child (UNCRC) 92, 98, 110

values 24-31, 37, 65, 69, 126; actionable 26, *26*; awareness of 25; convergence and divergence of *30*; definition of 24, 26; dynamic 26; educator *29*; evolving 26, *26*; expression of 25-6; importance of 25; institutional *48*, 50-1; life values *28*; living 26, *26*; multifaceted nature of 25-6; personal and professional 24; reflecting on 25; response 26; social media validation 81-2; soulful *26*, 27; uniqueness of 25, *26*; valuability *68*, *70*; values-based approach *17*, 20, 25, 26, *26*, 126; voice(s) *93*, 94, 101

voice(s) 18, 51, *68*, 69, *70*; audience 93; collaborative approach *93*, 95, 101; EDUCARE principles *93*, 93-5; embedding voices and participation in your learning environment *100*;

empowering 92-102; empowering through pedagogy **97**; enacted approach *93*, 95; five 'Ps' for voices in education 95-6, *96*; inclusive approach *93*, 94-5, 101; influence 93; learning environment for empowering voices audit *99*; Lundy's model of participation 93; physical space 96-8, 101; openhearted approach *93*, 94, 101; participation 96, 101; pedagogy 96, **97**, 101; policy 96, 98, 101; practices in education 96, 98, 101; supported approach *93*, 95, 101; valued approach *93*, 94, 101

voluntary work **57**

vulnerability *66*, 66-7, **106**, 110-11, **113**

war 2, 112

wellbeing 10, *10*, 13-4, 37, 45-60, 127-9, *128*; action plan *58*, *59*, 60; collective and individual 47; educators' relational *48*; emotional *17*; factors impacting upon *52*; negative 116; nurturing 53; physical *17*; positive 48-9; relational *48*, 50-1; time, space and place 48-9, *48*; tools and practices for educators **57**; *see also* Five Ways to Wellbeing framework; health; mental health

working culture 10, *10*, 15-6

Printed in the United States
by Baker & Taylor Publisher Services